Entrepreneurial
Finance

Taking Control of Your
Financial Decision Making

Robert
Ronstadt

Lord Publishing, Inc.
One Apple Hill
Suite 320
Natick, MA 01760
(508) 651-9955

Lord Publishing, Inc. is a twelve-year old company dedicated to providing books, software, case studies and other business tools to entrepreneurs. The company has developed the first of a family of personal computer software products designed exclusively for the needs of new and growing ventures.

Ronstadt's FINANCIALS™ is a trademark of Lord Publishing, Inc.

IBM PC, XT, AT and PC-DOS are registered trademarks of International Business Machines Corp. MS-DOS is a registered trademark of Microsoft Corporation.

Table of Contents

Acknowledgements

In her autobiography, *West With The Night*, the pioneering aviator, Beryl Markham, tells how her father created a working farm and mill from an East African forest during the early 19th century.

The farm at Njoro was endless, but it was no farm at all until my father made it. He made it out of nothing and out of everything — the things of which all farms are made. He made it out of forest and bush, rocks, new earth, sun, and torrents of warm rain. He made it out of labour and out of patience.

Beryl Markham,
West With The Night,
North Point Press,
San Francisco, CA, 1983, p. 67.

He also made it out of collaboration — with Englishmen, Dutchmen, Africans called Kavirondo and Kikuyu, all working together for endless hours. No one person ever creates anything of significant proportions without the help of others.

So it is with this book and its related software package, *Ronstadt's FINANCIALS* ... two items that are intertwined inseparably, the software being developed to make *Entrepreneurial Finance* a feasible activity for most entrepreneurs... and the book to help improve the quality of what gets put into the computer. They both bear my name, but the book and software have become a reality only because others worked with me.

Moreover, they worked "out in front." They didn't just follow. People often speak of "lead entrepreneurs leading," and lead they must; but anyone who's gone down the path of creating a high-growth venture knows that lead entrepreneurs must also be guided and supported in their choices.

And the choices have been many over the two and one-half years it has taken to create this book and its sister software product. Many choices have been difficult; others were simple, though not always easy to make or implement. Other choices simply took time, and sweat, and more time. If the literally thousands of choices have resulted in valuable products for society, the accolades belong mainly to those who helped make and implement them.

Let me start with the software, since that is where it all began.

It started first and foremost with my wife and partner, Rebecca Lord Ronstadt. The company bears her family name and rightly so, because she nurtured it for ten years before this latest project started. Her contributions touch every part of our current enterprise. She has shared all the highs and lows that come with the territory . . . the pressures, the worries, the sleepless nights. What we achieve, she has earned more than anyone.

Early in our enterprise, we were fortunate to meet Jim Moore, who, as head of the Center for Expert Systems, helped us to design *Ronstadt's FINANCIALS*. Jim brought Ann Lynnworth with him, one of the brightest, creative individuals I have known. Together they coaxed from me over six months some of the fundamental ideas that became the basis of our program. Later, they were joined by James Sprague whose keen and agile mind, coupled with solid training at MIT, helped shape the basic contours of our software program. James, together with Ann, translated these shapes and ideas into a functional design and programming code. They received considerable feedback from Walter Los who "exercised" the program by building some of our earliest industry financial models.

Subsequently, James Sprague joined Lord Publishing, Inc. full time as Manager of Product Development. Over the last six months, James has improved the final product greatly. Here he has been ably supported by Hae Yong Yi. While Hae greatly improved printing, George Mueller and Bob Powell of Level Zero, located in Wellesley, gave us an outstanding graphics capability that did not require an engineering degree to operate.

Over the last eight months, the fortunes of our software and book project improved immeasurably because of the contributions of Paul Conover. As Vice President of Sales and Marketing, Paul brought a wealth of experience in the software industry to Lord Publishing. Drawing on this experience, Paul helped greatly to refine our ideas about the market and our marketing. However, his contributions extended beyond marketing into product development and a number of other business areas. But Paul didn't stop here. Someone once said that "atmosphere is everything," and Paul Conover has made the atmosphere at Lord Publishing a fun and exciting one.

The day Barry Abrams came to work for Lord Publishing was a real turning point for our venture. As Chief Financial Officer, Barry kept us on course. Here he was supported ably by Lisa Torbin who expertly managed the accounting chores. Like Paul, Barry has helped us in many areas that went beyond his primary area of expertise. His considerable entrepreneurial experience served us well, especially during those inevitable crises when it's vital to have calm people around you. He also helped to refine my ideas in *Entrepreneurial Finance*, especially Chapter Five on "Understanding Your Financial Projections." But his crowning achievement has been the development of the industry "Library Files" in *Ronstadt's FINANCIALS*.

Janice Vocatura has worked for Lord Publishing almost from its inception twelve years ago. She is one of those rare and capable people whom one is continually asking, "What would we ever do without her." Her dedication and loyalty are the foundation upon which our venture is built.

Over the last six months, Nancy Libby has kept the entire operation humming smoothly, including our existing business. A top-notch administrator, Nancy makes things happen. When the detail became intense, she always came to the rescue.

Several people "outside" Lord Publishing made substantial contributions to the book and/or software. For instance, Barbara Huff of Simmons College wrote much of the "accounting glossary" contained in the software. Michael Sullivan of DesignSystems, worked tirelessly to infuse our software packaging, manual, and the *Entrepreneurial Finance* book with a physical design of exceptional quality. Les Boomhower, Annie Dewar, Chris Sylvia and James Bartlett of ZBR Publications, Inc. deserve special praise for helping us meet a demanding printing schedule. Their superlative work is reflected in the pages of *Entrepreneurial Finance* and the *User's Guide*.

A special tribute is made in memory of Aaron Zohn, President of ZBR Publications, Inc., who lived the American dream and personified entrepreneurial excellence.

I'd be remiss indeed if I failed to acknowledge Bill Hammond of Allied Consulting and Mason Fackert of The Concord Group who provided much sage advice about the strategic and financial issues that confronted us.

I also must thank the superb support of Jerry Fallon of New York who has helped me on several occasions to clarify my ideas. As always, Merrill Hassenfeld of Golub & Hassenfeld provided both sound legal counsel and the personal advice of a true friend. Similar support and wise insights have been tendered by Charles Sullivan, Sr., of Sullivan, Sorgi & Dimmock, and Dick O'Connor of O'Connor and Drew. Their respective partners, Peter Sorgi and James Drew, also made meaningful contributions along the way.

Dick Sears, the Director of the Center For Entrepreneurial Ventures, located in Portland, Oregon, was responsible for "firing us up" on several occasions with his infectious enthusiasm for our overall mission. He also contributed, along with his colleagues Deborah King and Hal Bergmann, some important insights about venture feasibility and ownership which helped to develop my thoughts about these subjects.

Graham Fallon of Kingsville, Maryland, deserves particular mention since his involvement played a major role in the development of both the software and the book almost from the beginning. His frequent visits to our home and offices always resulted in a better grasp of what had to be done. His encouragement for and review of

Entrepreneurial Finance made a big difference to me as I labored to complete the manuscript.

Finally, I am sure the book would still be incomplete and poorer in content without the professional and editorial guidance of my friend and colleague, Jeffrey Shuman of Bentley College. Not only did Jeff tirelessly nurture the creation of *Entrepreneurial Finance*, but he also worked to keep the entire enterprise on track and on schedule while helping to develop our seminar materials and our Venture Feasibility Workbook. His background as a practicing entrepreneur and educator proved invaluable ... not just with the conceptional development of *Entrepreneurial Finance* but the entire creative enterprise of book, software, and venture development.

Truly, Lord Publishing would not be what it is today without the help of these fine people plus the work of hundreds of others who've reviewed *Ronstadt's FINANCIALS*, *Entrepreneurial Finance*, or otherwise contributed to our venture.

To all of you, my heartfelt thanks. Like those who helped Beryl Markham's father, you've helped us create something that, hopefully, will be very good for entrepreneurs — something that was made "out of nothing and out of everything," and in the making, became something precious to us.

Bob Ronstadt
Natick, Massachusetts
January 1988

For Jane and Graham Fallon,
whose vision and trust
helped to create "this venture."

"When all is said and done, there are two kinds of people in the world: those who find a way to take control of their lives, and those who never do."

Albert Shapero
(1921 - 1985)
Scholar and pioneer in developing
the field of Entrepreneurial Studies

"'Maybe the knowledge is too great and maybe men are growing too small,' said Lee. 'Maybe, kneeling down to atoms, they're becoming atom-sized in their souls. Maybe a specialist is only a coward, afraid to look out of his little cage. And think what any specialist misses — the whole world over his fence.'"

John Steinbeck
East of Eden
Chapter 49, p. 438.

From Venture Planning to Superior Venture Thinking

'We always plan too much and always think too little.'

Joseph Schumpeter
Capitalism, Socialism and Democracy
(New York: Harper & Row, 1947), xi.

Introduction

This book is about the financial aspects of "venture thinking." It is also one of the first books to my knowledge that has been written expressly for and in conjunction with, the development of a major software program (called Ronstadt's FINANCIALS™). Nevertheless, the book stands on its own legs. You do not have to own the software to derive value from Entrepreneurial Finance. Both the book and software have been developed for entrepreneurs and venture planners with the recognition that the latter two are not always the same. I believe Entrepreneurial Finance and Ronstadt's FINANCIALS will prove very useful to many non-entrepreneurs. Nevertheless, my principal audience is entrepreneurs and those who aspire to become entrepreneurs. My goal is to convert two years of effort spent building the software program and writing this book into a package that represents a state-of-the-art approach to venture thinking...an approach that will help people to become more effective entrepreneurs by taking control of their financial decision making. If others benefit in the process, I will be doubly gratified.

Given this objective, a few words are appropriate to explain what I mean by venture planning and venture thinking. Let's discuss venture planning first and start by covering what it doesn't mean.

Here, I want to emphasize that venture planning is NOT exclusively about writing a "successful," "winning," "smashing," or otherwise "spectacular" business plan *per se*, although there is information in this book that will help you to produce an exceptional business plan. Nor is venture planning exclusively about producing financial projections for business plans, although again this book provides insights that will greatly assist you in generating these numbers. Both the book and software program are designed for venture planning which is concerned with more than the "back end" or the financial portion of business plans. Venture planning encompasses a broad range of planning activities that covers the life of an entrepreneurial venture.,

For instance, venture planning can include:

- *"Quick and dirty" feasibilities of new opportunities.* This pre-business plan work tells you if you should make the often significant investment of time (and money) in researching and writing a business plan. Venture feasibility analysis is a vital time saver that is critical not just for your first venture, but also for evaluating the new venture opportunities you will confront after starting your first venture. 1
- *The financial comparison of the numerous venture alternatives* that usually exist for each venture opportunity. Remember, busy loan officers, venture capitalists, or other investors do not want to consider your venture options. Deciding among an array of venture possibilities is your job.

- *The buildup of detailed schedules and budgets*, most of which should rarely be included in a business plan, but are nevertheless the necessary foundation upon which sound business plans rest, not to mention sound ventures.
- *The valuation of your venture at various points in its evolution, including before and after startup.* As we shall see, venture valuation can be used as a very effective decision making criterion for deciding among venture alternatives.
- *The development of expansion plans*, including the revision, and reuse of schedules, budgets, and financial projections for the purposes of expansion and diversification of a post-startup enterprise.

These distinctions about venture planning are worth making because my experience with a wide range of individuals, including students planning to become entrepreneurs, successful entrepreneurs, and even experts in the field of Entrepreneurial Studies, confirms that a serious confusion exists between the need for a business plan versus the need for venture planning.

Too often I hear that one doesn't really need a business plan... or if one is needed for financing purposes, then all you need to do is couple some appealing prose with vanilla coated financials. The rationale is that business plans are, at best, necessary evils ... misleading time wasters that are seldom followed and where the numbers rarely are the numbers that are realized anyway. From this position, the intellectual jump is just a short hop to a position where the individual's true feelings about planning surface; i.e., planning, any kind of planning, isn't all that necessary. The supporting line usually goes something like this: "After all, what 's really important is to get out there and make it happen." Unfortunately, precisely what "it" is remains all too often vague and ill-defined.

Should this claim sound outlandish, let me remind you that there is a popular school of thought (perhaps a better word is "myth") that the sufficient conditions for entrepreneurial success are an ability to take action, pound the pavement, and be a good dealmaker. These are certainly positive traits, but they are hardly sufficient for long-N term success. Positive traits do not insure entrepreneurial success. They simply aren't enough, despite the claims of many a venture capitalist. More than good people are required to make a successful venture. I used to think that an "A" entrepreneur could make a "B" venture fly. But I don't anymore. Over the years, my experience has taught me that failed ventures are just as often the product of errors in concept, errors in strategy, or errors in planning, as much as they are errors in execution. So let's get our facts straight. Sometimes a new venture does NOT require a business plan. Sometimes, even when a business plan is advisable, an entrepreneur can experience success without one. 2 However, rarely, if ever, is it possible to realize a successful venture or expand an existing one without doing some good old fashioned venture planning. In many instances, this venture planning does not result in a written document. But the absence of a document, especially a formal business plan, should not be taken as evidence that planning is not occurring.

In addition, venture planning is NOT necessarily "formal organizational planning." The latter often involves other members of an organization, who follow some prescribed planning procedure. The most successful entrepreneurs I know, specifically those who have been successful over a decade or more, are ardent venture planners . . . which is to say they spend a great deal of time *thinking* about their entrepreneurial activities. But many of them don't have a staff of planners. Nor do they always write or talk about their venture plans. But they do think hard about the longer term consequences of their actions. Each of these individuals knows, at least intuitively, that they can go to war and fight a battle without a plan, but the risks involved and the potential negative consequences argue for some hard thinking about strategy and tactics, even if these must be discarded as events unfold. Sometimes events force them to fight without the luxury of a plan. But, given a choice, I don't know many savvy entrepreneurs, or generals for that matter, who advise "winging it."

Fortunately, most entrepreneurs have no real need to "wing it." Quite the contrary, they can hardly afford to bypass the "necessary luxury" of planning, even if they're bad at it, or even if they disbelieve its value. Superior ventures are usually the recipients of superior venture planning. Let me say as clearly as I can: *every* venture requires venture planning that represents serious thinking about the venture itself and how the venture will realize its long term mission.

How then does an entrepreneur become a "superior venture thinker?" You start by spending time identifying and evaluating the basic ways to create, grow, stabilize, and possibly sell, go public, or otherwise harvest a venture. Such thinking involves not only logical analysis but also creative thinking. Superior venture thinking then goes one step further: it converts these options into financial scenarios. Superior venture thinking means being able to identify and compare each "basic way" or venture scenario and determine which is the best for you and/or your venture. The predominant means of comparison (but not exclusive nor always definitive) is through comparisons of future financial performance.

Such financial comparisons provide answers to questions such as: Which venture scenario produces the most sales, the best margins, the highest net profit, the lowest breakeven? ... Which scenario requires the least investment by you, or by others? Which scenario requires equity, as opposed to debt financing? Which produces the highest "return on investment," the best liquidity, or which requires you to give up the least equity? Superior venture thinking is concerned with these and other questions.

As with any human endeavor, you can spend too much time thinking about your venture at the expense of getting things accomplished. It is also true that successful ventures are never realized without effective execution. Balance is everything, whether it be a balanced entrepreneurial team, a balanced set of financial resources, or a delicate balance between thinking and acting. Nevertheless, you need to know more than simple admonitions about a balanced approach to superior venture thinking. How much venture thinking is enough? When is it overdone? When is "quick and dirty" planning actually superior venture thinking?

Venture Evolution and Venture Thinking

I believe knowing something about the evolution of a venture can help you to determine how much venture thinking is appropriate. This evolution is shown in Diagram 1. It shows the key phases in the early evolution of a venture and the kind of venture thinking that is appropriate at each phase. The diagram also highlights the fact that financial projections and budgets are the foundation upon which superior venture thinking rests, regardless of when it occurs.

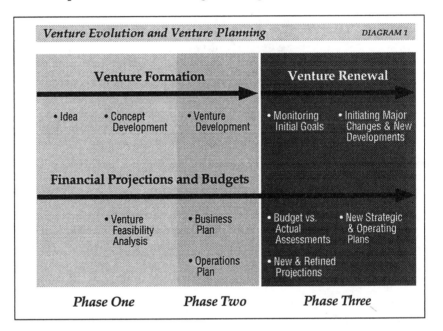

There are two additional events that Diagram 1 overlooks that nevertheless impact entrepreneurs as their ventures evolve. The first is more obvious because it is consistent with the kind of linear thinking that often entraps us. It is the need to think about the ultimate disposition of a venture. This disposition may include discontinuing the venture, selling it to other private parties, a public offering, and/or succession.

The second event is less obvious because it often takes us off the linear progression of events we've been following and puts us on a new pathway. Strong empirical evidence now exists that many entrepreneurs get involved in more than one venture, often very early in the life of their first venture. 3 And for those who pursue only one venture throughout their entrepreneurial careers, the likelihood exists they will witness one or more "venture rebirths" as their venture moves in new directions that require yet a new round of venture thinking.

Entrepreneurial careers exist, and they are composed of many startups. Sometimes these startups are "ventures within ventures." We witness no new legal entity but something new has been created. At other times, new legal entities do emerge, sometimes before the prior venture is ended, at other times, after it. But for every new venture, many more venture opportunities are evaluated and discarded. In each instance, financial projections are needed, albeit in varying degrees of refinement, for each phase of a venture's evolution.

Here are some observations about each phase.

Phase #1

Opportunity Evaluation and Concept Development

When you identify a venture opportunity, your first step is NOT to write a business plan but to do a venture feasibility analysis. As you will appreciate in a moment, a venture feasibility will save you considerable time, while helping to insure that you will make a sound decision either to go ahead with or drop the proposed idea.

The Venture Feasibility Process, unlike the Business Plan, is a very informal and personal process, in many cases "for your eyes only." You don't need an extensive document nor detailed projections, but you do need some ballpark figures to tell you if the venture is within your financial capabilities.

The time it takes to do a venture feasibility assessment ranges from 35 to 70 hours depending on the circumstances.

Phase #2

Venture Formation

Once a feasible venture concept is identified, the next step is to produce a business plan or an operations plan. The average time to create a business plan (including field research) is usually cited at about 300 hours. Unfortunately, averages can lie. The actual time will vary widely depending on the scope and type of venture you are considering. My experience and experience of others who have actually had to write these plans ranges from 100 hours to nearly 2000 hours. 4

The low end usually involves routine one person operations that are income substituting ventures requiring little or no up front investment. The high end of the spectrum are complex, high growth ventures that often require significant startup capital and time … a year or more of pre-marketing and product development work before you can open the doors for business.

Phase #3

Venture Renewal

Serious venture thinking should occur almost continually once a venture is started. Circumstances will dictate when this thinking should be conducted in a more formal fashion. Obviously, one simply doesn't have the time to continually write new business plans as a venture is developing. However, serious and proactive rounds of venture planning cannot be ignored when:

- major expansions of the existing venture are possible
- the existing venture can be taken in new directions
- considering the feasibility and appropriateness of new venture opportunities.

Guidelines for Superior Venture Thinking

Regardless of when venture thinking occurs, there are certain guidelines in developing financial strategy, projections, and budgets that help promote truly superior venture thinking. These guidelines are:

Guideline #1

Superior venture thinking means identifying the major options for starting or expanding a venture.

This guideline is particularly appropriate during Phase One. My experience is that too many entrepreneurs lock into a single venture concept much too early during the formation stage.

A fundamental goal of venture feasibility analysis is to identify the different options or ways to pursue a venture opportunity.

Guideline #2

Superior venture thinking means understanding your assumptions for each major option.

To aid "future-oriented" decision making, experienced entrepreneurs and managers attempt to observe the impact of both current and future decisions on financial results that are estimated to occur next week, next month, next year, or even farther into the future. What will be the impact of decisions to increase inventory, lower price, and increase advertising on future sales, profits, and cash flow? If current assumptions are changed about wage levels, manpower availability, interest rates, effective tax rates, how does it affect a projected income statement, balance sheet, and cash flow?

Anytime one or more assumptions are changed, the effects ripple through all the statements and produce a new financial "scenario" for your consideration. Comparing and selecting the most realistic scenarios is a fundamental task for the leader of any enterprise. But given the uncertainties of life and the marketplace, prudent leaders also need to know how to manage the impact of pessimistic and optimistic scenarios. Here it is ever so easy to avoid or delay decisions because you do not appreciate fully the consequences.

For instance, cutting personnel is seldom an easy task. No one enjoys telling a good employee that they must be let go for the sake of the firm. Just how long can you prudently wait before taking such action? What other cutbacks are possible? How far can sales decline before you must take action without jeopardizing the jobs of others? Responsible leaders use assumption making and financial scenario planning to help them make these difficult but crucial decisions.

Guideline #3

Superior venture thinking means producing and evaluating alternative financial projections for each major option <u>before</u> you write the final draft of your business plan or other plans.

Most business plans discuss financial strategies toward the end of the document. A few comments may be made in the beginning about capital needs and financial objectives but, by and large, the financial meat and potatoes are offered after discussions of the team, the market, the product, and operations. The financial projections supporting the financial and business strategies are usually relegated even farther to the rear, in an appendix.

From a presentation standpoint, I have no argument with this or-dering of material. It is quite appropriate. It does, however, mask a very fundamental point about the process of venture planning, and, in this example, the process of creating a superior business plan. The point is that the " back of the business plan" actually determines much of what you say or can say in the earlier portions. It not only determines WHAT you have to say, but also affects greatly the QUALITY of what you have to say.

I've read many business plans and rarely have I seen:

- A strong and convincing front portion (let's say 80% of the initial text) when the back portion, especially the financials, has been su-perficial or otherwise weak.
- A weak front portion when the back end; i.e., the financials, are strong.

Because the financials touch every part of the business plan, you need to button them up before writing your final draft. All too many budding entrepreneurs tend to write the text portions of the business plan first and then "add on" or append the projections. This observation does NOT mean you should let your financials deter-mine your marketing and business strategy. Quite the contrary. The strategy process is an iterative one. Just don't leave the financial work for last.

Guideline #4

Clearly understanding and documenting your assumptions for each finan-cial scenario (i.e., set of financial projections) you produce.

Your financial projections will be meaningless to others if you don't clearly explain your assumptions. Furthermore, they will quickly become meaningless to you with the passage of time. Ven-ture thinking is only as good as your assumptions, and superior ven-ture thinking requires superior assumptions.

The first step is to identify and to understand your assumptions. Unfortunately, the power of today's electronic spreadsheets have helped us to forget them.

The second step is to document them.

Guideline #5
Superior venture thinking means coupling "top down" planning with strong "bottom up" planning.

Strong bottom up planning means producing detailed budgets and schedules that build up the key line items of your Sales Forecast, Income Statement, and Balance Sheet. Such detail is important when venture thinking must become more formalized venture planning. Critical numbers must be qualified, not plucked from thin air.

Guideline #6:
Superior venture thinking means simplifying your financial projections so you can retain them and use them to monitor your venture.

Detailed work is often needed during the venture formation phase and the venture renewal phase. It can give you insight and confidence. It can mean the difference between being properly capitalized or undercapitalized. It can also get you and others lost. Consequently, it is vital to simplify your work. Simplification promotes understanding. It also promotes utility. Very few of us can retain great detail for very long. One week after your concluding session with your venture capitalist you will have forgotten 80% of the details associated with your financials. What you must retain, however, are the basic relationships and the key numbers. So, simplify your work.

On Financial Projections and Superior Venture Thinking

Superior venture thinking is future thinking. One way, perhaps the best way, to convert future thinking into meaningful financial terms is to assemble financial projections.

Two general classes of financial statements exist: accounting statements and financial projections. Accounting statements include balance sheets, income statements, cash flow statements, plus other statements that show the actual performance of an enterprise for and over some period of time. It is important to realize that financial projections or proforma statements are also balance sheets, income statements, and cash flow statements that can be identical in every way to accounting statements except one . . . projections represent estimates of future performance rather than "actual" historical performance, as shown in Diagram 2.

To recognize this difference, some professionals like to refer to accounting statements as "statements" while referring to financial projections as "proforma" or "financials." This distinction is important for someone reading a set of statements who may otherwise confuse projections for actual, historical performance. But, for our purposes, convenience dictates an interchangeable use of the word "statements" for both historic and future numbers.

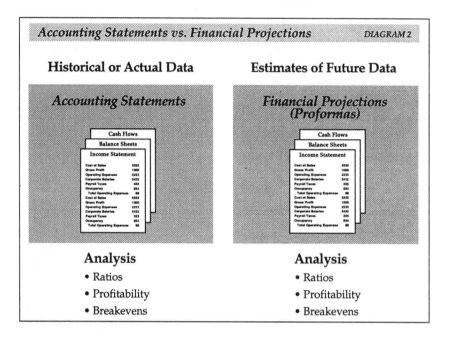

Accounting Statements vs. Financial Projections   DIAGRAM 2

Historical or Actual Data   **Estimates of Future Data**

Accounting Statements   *Financial Projections (Proformas)*

Analysis   **Analysis**
- Ratios   • Ratios
- Profitability   • Profitability
- Breakevens   • Breakevens

There is one critical distinction about historical versus proforma statements worth making at this time. It is important to realize that entrepreneurs and many managers possess a need for financial information that extends beyond the information provided by traditional accounting statements. As records of historical performance, accounting statements serve nicely the needs of stockholders and many managers of larger corporations. But they are insufficient vehicles for decision making, particularly when entrepreneurial decisions must be made about the creation or expansion of a venture.

This insufficiency is apparent for new ventures since there is no history of past performance, at least until the venture incurs some costs. Even then the utility of accounting statements is limited for making future decisions until the venture has a sales history ... a fact not lost on many "ventureless venture capitalists" who simply refuse to invest in any company without a sales history.

But entrepreneurial decisions have to be made before a sales history emerges. And once it emerges, more decisions must be made under uncertain and changing conditions that disallow the simple one-to-one correlation of the future with the past. Entrepreneurial decision makers need more than historical accounting statements. They need future oriented statements or projections to help them make decisions now, which will have an impact later.

Organization of This Book and "Ronstadt's FINANCIALS"

The relationship between and importance of financial projections for superior venture thinking is covered in the first three chapters of this book. These chapters also describe why existing approaches and tools have been less than satisfactory. Regretfully, the current barriers to developing good financial projections have successfully defeated the vast majority of entrepreneurs. Hence, the reason for the creation of the software program, Ronstadt's FINANCIALS.*

From the outset, Ronstadt's FINANCIALS was designed and developed by entrepreneurs for other entrepreneurs who are neither financial experts nor computer experts. Ronstadt's FINANCIALS overcomes the barriers of producing financial projections by providing a library of pre-defined financial models for several different industries. (See Diagram 3) This means that your projections are already preformatted and, more importantly, all the formulas are written that are needed to produce an accurate set of projections. You only need to enter the values for some underlying assumptions to generate a complete set of financial projections that includes a sales forecast, income statement, balance sheet, and cash flow statement.

The program comes with seven financial models plus a personal finance model (because the line between a venture's financial status and an entrepreneur's personal financial condition is, more often than not, a very thin one). Other financial models, representing different industries and/or more detail, are available from Lord Publishing. The seven financial models are ideal for *venture feasibility analysis* and can be modified to perform more detailed venture planning.

*For IBM PCs and compatibles.

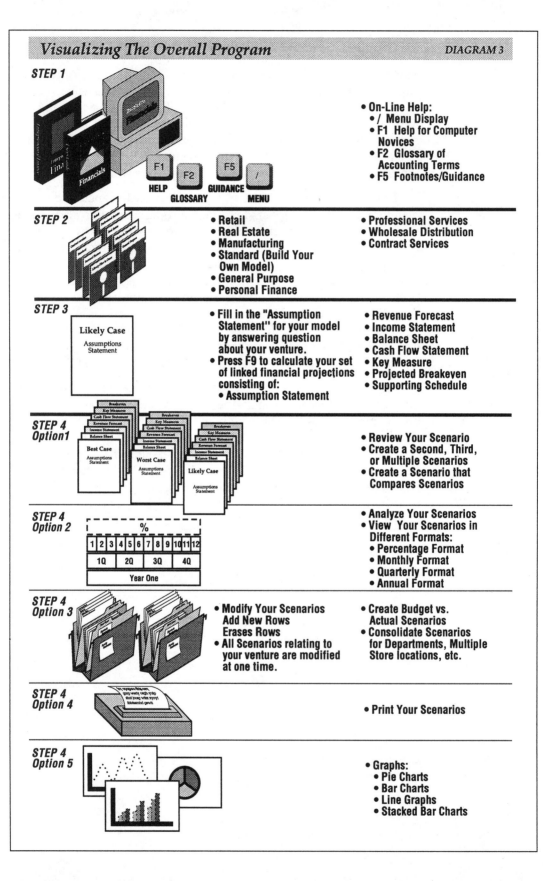

Visualizing The Overall Program   DIAGRAM 3

STEP 1

- On-Line Help:
  - / Menu Display
  - F1 Help for Computer Novices
  - F2 Glossary of Accounting Terms
  - F5 Footnotes/Guidance

F1 HELP   F2 GLOSSARY   F5 GUIDANCE   / MENU

STEP 2

- Retail
- Real Estate
- Manufacturing
- Standard (Build Your Own Model)
- General Purpose
- Personal Finance

- Professional Services
- Wholesale Distribution
- Contract Services

STEP 3

Likely Case

Assumptions Statement

- Fill in the "Assumption Statement" for your model by answering question about your venture.
- Press F9 to calculate your set of linked financial projections consisting of:
  - Assumption Statement

- Revenue Forecast
- Income Statement
- Balance Sheet
- Cash Flow Statement
- Key Measure
- Projected Breakeven
- Supporting Schedule

STEP 4 Option 1

Best Case
Assumptions Statement

Worst Case
Assumptions Statement

Likely Case
Assumptions Statement

- Review Your Scenario
- Create a Second, Third, or Multiple Scenarios
- Create a Scenario that Compares Scenarios

STEP 4 Option 2

%

| 1 | 2 | 3 | 4 | 5 | 6 | 7 | 8 | 9 | 10 | 11 | 12 |

| 1Q | 2Q | 3Q | 4Q |

Year One

- Analyze Your Scenarios
- View Your Scenarios in Different Formats:
  - Percentage Format
  - Monthly Format
  - Quarterly Format
  - Annual Format

STEP 4 Option 3

- Modify Your Scenarios
  Add New Rows
  Erases Rows
- All Scenarios relating to your venture are modified at one time.

- Create Budget vs. Actual Scenarios
- Consolidate Scenarios for Departments, Multiple Store locations, etc.

STEP 4 Option 4

- Print Your Scenarios

STEP 4 Option 5

- Graphs:
  - Pie Charts
  - Bar Charts
  - Line Graphs
  - Stacked Bar Charts

Ronstadt's FINANCIALS also provides an intuitive menu system that allows:

- Extensive on line help for all accounting and finance terms used in the program. If you can't remember what an "acid test ratio" is, just press a single key and a definition, examples, and/or guidelines are presented.

- Extensive footnoting of every item plus a capability to document fully each statement and financial scenario.

- An orderly documentation of all assumptions in one concise statement.

- Extensive budgeting capability. You can produce supporting budgets and schedules that feed into your financial projections or "nest" an unlimited number of subrows within the projections themselves. Each "nested subrow" automatically sums up to its parent row.

- Multiple scenarios (worst, likely, best, etc.) can be compared on the computer screen at the same time.

- Monthly statements converted into quarterly or annual statements at the touch of a key.

- Percentages, ratios, breakevens, scenario consolidation, and more at the touch of a key.

- Single keystroke printing of selected lines, entire statements, entire scenarios, selected formulas, or all formulas (which are written in English).

- Single keystroke graphing that produces pie, bar, stacked bar, and line graphs in high resolution color (for those with a color monitor and EGA graphics card).

Most importantly, Ronstadt's FINANCIALS is designed to handle changes in these financial models should you wish to make them. We've discovered that many changes are relatively simple. More substantive changes, especially those that require new formulas, mean you need to know something about how financial projections are put together in the first place. Consequently, the middle chapters (4 & 5) present the basics of financial projections. Chapter 4 is especially important because it emphasizes the critical role of assumptions and creative assumption making.

Once a set of financial projections is created, the next difficulty some entrepreneurs have is interpreting and presenting the output. Regarding interpretation, Chapters 6 - 9 deal with ways to find the best answers to the five key questions of Entrepreneurial Finance: **How much money does your venture need? When do you need this money? What kind of money should you seek? Where should you seek these funds? and, What value should be placed on them?**

Regarding the simplification and presentation of your venture's financial needs, Chapter 10 offers some insight about how to communicate your findings to different groups. Chapter 11 discusses the link between entrepreneurial success and your ability to make financial projections and understand them.

All of this information is designed to help you take control of your financial decision making. You will have to invest some time to gain this control. But I believe the returns will justify your efforts as you move from venture planning to superior venture thinking.

Endnotes

1 The rationale and procedure for a venture feasibility approach to venture creation and expansion is explained in *Venture Feasibility Planning Guide: Your First Step Before Writing a Business Plan*, Robert Ronstadt and Jeffrey Shuman, Lord Publishing, Inc., Natick, Massachusetts, 1988.

2 About half of the Inc. 500 never wrote a formal business plan; however, nearly all allocated significant time to "planning activities." About 84% felt strategic planning was useful or highly useful. See Shuman, Sussman, and Shaw's "Business Plan and The Startup of Rapid Growth Companies," *Frontiers of Entrepreneurship Research,* 1985, Center for Entrepreneurial Studies, Babson College, Wellesley, Ma. 1985, pp. 294-313.

3 The data come from a survey of 1,537 independent entrepreneurs who were founders, cofounders, or lead entrepreneurs. A unique aspect of the study is that it included 163 "ex-entrepreneurs" (people who were working full time for someone else). To the best of my knowledge, this group of ex-entrepreneurs is the largest number of "failed" entrepreneurs ever identified. The study showed that 63% of the practicing entrepreneurs had created at least a second venture by the time of the survey versus 40% for the ex-entrepreneurs. See Robert Ronstadt, "The Corridor Principle," *Journal of Business Venturing,* Winter, 1988.

4 One expert notes that "Business Plans are comprehensive documents which often require several months to compile." See Joseph R. Mancuso, *How to Start, FINANCE, and Manage Your Own Small Business,* Prentice Hall, Englewood, New Jersey, 1978, p. 70. I should note that "several months" translates into 720 hours assuming an "average" entrepreneur's work week of six days, ten hours per day, for three months. Also, these hours are usually stretched out over a longer period of time for those who cannot afford a full time effort prior to the startup of their venture.

Entrepreneurial Finance: What Is It?

1

1

The Current Dilemma

All of the following stories happened. Only some names and other identifying factors have been changed to protect the protagonists who dropped all pretenses and spoke the truth for our benefit. Neither are these stories unusual. Rather, I believe they represent the experiences of many people who have become lost in the forest of accounting and finance and/or the midnight forest of spreadsheet cells and formulas. In either instance, they represent disappointment and failure to obtain control over a critical entrepreneurial activity … financial decision making.

> *In early 1985, Tom Mitchell had co-founded a new advertising firm that was off to a good start. However, he needed to develop some financial projections for his business and he needed them fast if he was going to obtain a small equity investment from a friend in order to expand operations. Using a traditional spreadsheet, Tom eventually developed a full set of financial projections. But he never presented these particular projections to his investor because they took him six months to create. Even more discouraging was the fact that the resulting model was so complicated that Tom had a hard time using it. Tom's partner was never able to fathom Tom's financial model, much less use it to generate new projections. In fact, he doesn't trust the output that Tom gives him. Neither does Tom.*

> *Mary Kinkaid had a similar but somewhat more embarrassing experience. For years Mary had dreamed about starting a small retail business. And she had finally realized her dream. Using her savings and some investment money she raised, Mary had opened her store. Once in business, she felt she could get a small working capital loan from her local bank.*
>
> *"Up to this point I'd put together a few simple figures for my business plan. Nothing fancy. Just some sales forecasts and a proforma P&L. I knew the bank wanted more.*
>
> *Unfortunately I got all balled up when I tried to add a balance sheet and cash flow and link them all together, so when I changed some variable — for instance, the amount of inventory purchases — then everything else would change automatically. I was led to believe my spreadsheet could handle this kind of work. I suppose it could if I became a power user and devoted all my time to doing projections. But I just didn't have the time. All I knew was that my simple spreadsheet wasn't so simple anymore. It contained several errors which I didn't catch. My loan officer, unfortunately, was more observant."*

Apparently, being a "power user" isn't enough either, as the experience of David Travis suggests.

Dave was in the investment banking business and his work required him to become proficient with personal computers and spreadsheets. So when his wife decided to start an antique business, it was natural for Dave to offer his support with the financial side of the venture, including the development of a full set of financial projections with detailed budgets for equipment purchases.

What Dave discovered next was that he wasn't an accountant. While he'd spent years analyzing financials, he'd never had to develop a full set of projections before where the balance sheet, income statement, and cash flow were all linked together. "The truth of the matter was that after spending about 60 hours on this project, I just couldn't get the balance sheet to balance. At that point I knew it would probably take me another 60 hours to figure out what was wrong. So I decided 'to fudge it' and hope the bank wouldn't look too closely."

Jim Allison took a completely different approach to financial decision making for his venture. His answer was to ignore the task. Unfortunately, his failure to consider some numbers about the future course of his business led to disaster. Because he ran his business by the seat of his pants, he went out of business. Jim didn't have the time or ability to do the numbers manually ... and he sure didn't have time to learn about computers. He's got plenty of time now.

Sam Jameison was just the opposite of Jim. Sam liked numbers and it was not an overstatement to say he was in love with his spreadsheet program. He spent six months learning to become reasonably proficient with the program, along with several hundred dollars for special training classes. Sam also had a new business that was growing and needed significant expansion money.

Sam decided to try and raise this money from the venture capital community. However, he never got to first base. Armed with a business plan that contained over 40 pages of folded, 11" by 17" spreadsheets, Sam never made it past the initial screen of several venture capital companies.

Sam later discovered he wasn't passing the "oh hum" test ... or as one venture capitalist put it, "We get 600 business plans in here each year. The first thing I do when I get one is to open to the exhibits. If I see too many spreadsheets, I say "oh hum" and toss it in the wastebasket. You usually can't trace the underlying logic and math. I simply don't have the time to do an audit."

While each of these stories is different, what all of the protagonists have in common is a need for a working knowledge of Entrepreneurial Finance and a better way to apply this knowledge than the conventional spreadsheet.

I have two reasons for writing this book. My primary purpose is to explain what one needs to know about financial decision making for new and expanding ventures. Here the objective is to provide you with a basic understanding of those elements of finance, accounting, and budgeting that will increase your odds of successfully creating, running, and/or expanding a venture.

My second reason is to demonstrate how to use a new software tool I have developed with the help of many other experts which, for the first time, provides a mechanism for decision makers to take control of their financial destinies without overly (and unfairly) relying on accountants, financial analysts, and/or computer analysts. This software program, called Ronstadt's FINANCIALS, is designed to let NON-financial and NON-computer experts apply the basic techniques of Entrepreneurial Finance. As the real examples narrated above suggest, prior to the development of this program, applying the tools of Entrepreneurial Finance was no easy task.

What Is Entrepreneurial Finance?

Entrepreneurial Finance consists of knowing how to identify, develop, and implement the appropriate financial strategies needed to create and operate a new venture or significantly expand an existing enterprise. While Entrepreneurial Finance is useful primarily to new venture decision makers, it can be applied by any enterprising person or group that seeks to understand the financial implications of some action they are considering.

Faced with critical venture decisions, enterprising people need to know which financial questions and numbers are the appropriate ones. Then they need to know how to use and interpret these numbers to make important venture decisions about relevant financial strategies for new venture creation, as well as realistic sources of funds.

Entrepreneurial Finance is not Corporate Finance. The latter is a worthwhile subject that is taught in most business schools, but it is largely irrelevant to most entrepreneurs. The financial strategies and financial sources available to the vast majority of entrepreneurs differ greatly from those strategies and sources available to established and larger corporations.

Some elements of what I call Entrepreneurial Finance are also taught in existing business courses. But they are often buried within six or seven hundred pages of material that covers a variety of topics more pertinent to the financial administration of Fortune 500 companies.

More importantly, these courses and books rarely give any treatment to the development of financials and budgets starting from ground zero. Nearly always there is an ABC Company that has historical finance and accounting statements. The accounting notion of an ongoing business is assumed with few exceptions. Entrepreneurial Finance makes just the opposite assumption. There is no financial history. We are starting from scratch.

Why You Need to Learn Entrepreneurial Finance

People who engage in venture creation, development, and expansion require financial resources. But how much is needed, when the money is needed, where to get these funds, and how much to pay for them (in interest, fees, and equity) is not usually clear … even when it seems clear.

The cost involved in raising money (both in terms of time and actual dollar outlays) is often undervalued or ignored until it becomes all too obvious. However, this cost can be substantial, especially when the venture possesses large up-front investment requirements and/or significant growth expectations.

Both reasons, the inevitable need for funds (even if the funds are your own) and the cost of raising them, require entrepreneurs and other enterprising people to learn about Entrepreneurial Finance.

Beyond these reasons is the sobering observation that a very large number of all discontinued businesses are closed down each year simply because they run out of money. The history of entrepreneurship is replete with instances of extraordinarily successful enterprises that barely survived a cash crunch just when they were starting. Of course, there are a large number of causes that result in a financial crisis and discontinuance, and not all of these can be avoided just by better financial planning; however, a good share can be avoided, especially during the early startup of a new venture.

Effective financial planning does not mean raising every dollar you can get your hands on. The illusory solution to running out of money is to raise much more than is needed. Such financial cushions also carry a high price. The price can be loss of control or an equity position that no longer provides incentive to the entrepreneur but gives all the incentive in the world to walk away from the venture. Other devastating effects of "overcapitalization" are discussed in the next chapter.

The principal rule of Entrepreneurial Finance is that effective financial planning means being neither undercapitalized nor overcapitalized. It means finding what I call the threshold band of capitalization at critical points in the life of your venture so you can determine how much money you need to raise. (See Diagram 1-1)

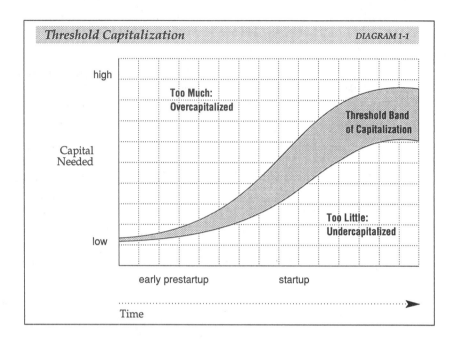

Threshold Capitalization   DIAGRAM 1-1

How Ronstadt's FINANCIALS Represents a New Breakthrough

It's one thing to tell people they "should" learn Entrepreneurial Finance. It's quite another matter to give them the tools to apply what they learn. Up to this point applying the concepts of Entrepreneurial Finance has been, practically speaking, impossible for most people. That's why Ronstadt's FINANCIALS represents an important breakthrough for the application of Entrepreneurial Finance.

Ronstadt's FINANCIALS is the first tool to give non-specialists the opportunity to use linked financial projections and budgets without the aid of accounting-computer experts ... to truly take control of their financial decision making. Ronstadt's FINANCIALS has been designed and developed by experts in entrepreneurship, accounting and finance to help you answer the key questions of Entrepreneurial Finance. The program assists you in determining how much money you will need to start and/or expand a venture. It helps you determine when you will need this money and, indirectly, where to find it (given answers to the "how much" and "when" questions). It helps you to avoid being undercapitalized or overcapitalized.

Non-specialists can take advantage of pre-defined financial statements representing many different industries. Each set of financial statements was organized and formatted by experts and then linked together with pre-defined formulas. (See Diagram 1-2)

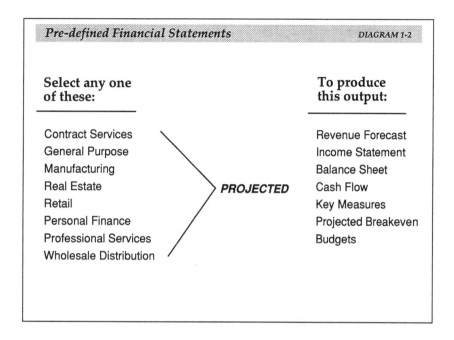

Pre-defined Financial Statements   *DIAGRAM 1-2*

**Select any one
of these:**

Contract Services
General Purpose
Manufacturing
Real Estate   **PROJECTED**
Retail
Personal Finance
Professional Services
Wholesale Distribution

**To produce
this output:**

Revenue Forecast
Income Statement
Balance Sheet
Cash Flow
Key Measures
Projected Breakeven
Budgets

What this linkage means is that you can see the effects of a great many "what if" changes. For instance, "what if" my sales are higher than expected, or "what if" I decide to spend more money on R&D, marketing, or add new employees? Ronstadt's FINANCIALS automatically calculates the effects of such changes not only on the statement where you make the change but on all other statements. Everything is linked together. 1

Ronstadt's FINANCIALS also helps non-financial people to understand finance and accounting terms through an extensive glossary of terms. Additional "help screens" assist non-experts to understand the financial implications of results they obtain.

In addition, Ronstadt's FINANCIALS is the first program that allows you to observe multiple financial situations at the same time. For instance, you can compare Budget versus Actual Results or Likely, Worst, and Best Case projections and see their financial ramifications in either graphic or printed output WITHOUT switching between files or pasting together printed output from different spreadsheets. (See Diagrams 1-3A and 1-3B)

Income Statement: Worst Software Venture   DIAGRAM 1-3A

```
                        Income Statement
                  Worst        Software Venture


                                        Qtr 1        Qtr 1        Qtr 1
                                        Worst        Likely       Best
                                      -----------  -----------  -----------
Net Sales.....................        $535,925     $1,274,760   $2,383,200
Cost of Sales.................        $63,050      $114,728     $198,600
                                      -----------  -----------  -----------
Gross Profit..................        $472,875     $1,160,032   $2,184,600
                                      -----------  -----------  -----------
Operating Expenses:
   Payroll expense............        $236,438     $236,438     $236,438
   Sales Commissions..........        $80,389      $127,476     $357,480
   Shipping expenses..........        $7,881       $13,240      $33,100
   Depreciation ..............        $3,583       $3,583       $3,583
   Office expenses............        $150,000     $150,000     $150,000
                                      -----------  -----------  -----------
   Total operating expenses...        $478,291     $530,736     $780,601
                                      -----------  -----------  -----------
Operating Profit (Loss).......        $(5,416)     $629,296     $1,403,999
Interest Expense..............        $1,311       $1,311       $1,311
                                      -----------  -----------  -----------
Net Income (Loss).............        $(6,727)     $627,985     $1,402,688
                                      ===========  ===========  ===========
```

Graph of Net Sales for Multiple Scenarios   DIAGRAM 1-3B

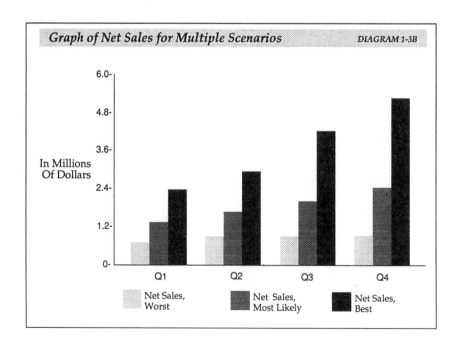

A Few Key Terms

For clarity's sake, there are a few terms I should define since they can have several interpretations. In this book, the terms "entrepreneur" and "entrepreneurship" refer specifically to one or more individuals directly engaged in the creation of a new venture. By "creation" I do not mean a specific point in time; e.g., the day an enterprise opens its doors for business. Rather, creation refers to a span of time that can vary greatly from one venture to the next. This varying span of time starts with the conception of an idea for a venture to the point where the venture is firmly established. (See Diagram 1-4)

The time it takes to create a new venture is divided into two parts. The first is the PRESTARTUP PERIOD which extends from the conception of the venture idea to the day you open your doors for business. The second part is the STARTUP PERIOD which extends from the startup date to the date the venture is firmly established. These distinctions are important because they have a direct bearing on several key issues of Entrepreneurial Finance. 2

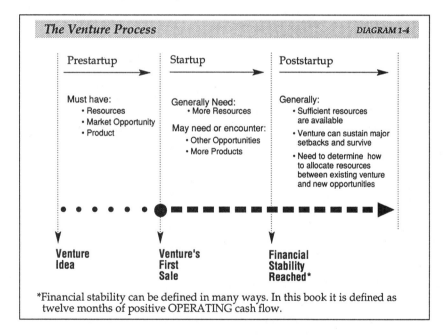

The Venture Process   *DIAGRAM 1-4*

Prestartup → | Startup → | Poststartup →

Must have:
• Resources
• Market Opportunity
• Product

Generally Need:
• More Resources

May need or encounter:
• Other Opportunities
• More Products

Generally:
• Sufficient resources are available
• Venture can sustain major setbacks and survive
• Need to determine how to allocate resources between existing venture and new opportunities

Venture Idea | **Venture's First Sale** | **Financial Stability Reached***

*Financial stability can be defined in many ways. In this book it is defined as twelve months of positive OPERATING cash flow.

Another key term is the word "VENTURE". I intentionally did not use the word "business" in most of the text because the need for financial projections, budgets, and schedules include nonbusiness ventures such as charitable organizations, foundations, or other kinds of nonprofit corporations. A venture may also involve the creation or operation of social and community organizations, municipalities, or other government agencies and departments that require financial decision making.

Or a venture may even be a personal one. Personal income statements, balance sheets, and cash flows can help you to decide if this is the year a new home or other major purchase can be made. In fact, one of the first uses of Ronstadt's FINANCIALS was by one of our programmers who used an early test version to see if his "personal cash flow" could sustain the purchase of a new car. It did.

In this book, I will talk about three very different kinds of ventures: *Lifestyle Ventures, Smaller Hi-Profit Ventures, and High Growth Ventures*. All three types of ventures can be defined roughly in terms of sales and employee ranges. For instance:

Type of Venture	Sales Range	Employees
Lifestyle	0 to $1,000,000	0 to 4
Smaller Hi-Profit	$1 to $20 million	5 to 50
High Growth	Over $20 million	Over 50

These relationships are shown in Diagram 1-5.

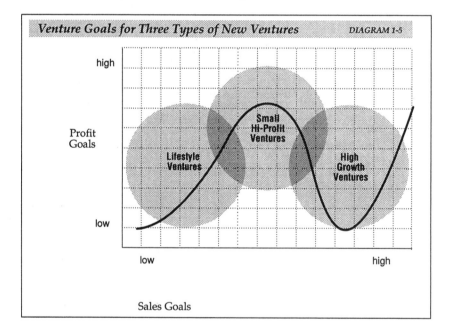

I want to emphasize that these cutpoints are not sharp or definitive. Work is still being done on where to draw the line and we already know that overlap can exist. 3 Also, other factors are important when defining each of these ventures besides sales and employee levels. For instance, Lifestyle Ventures are started by entrepreneurs who wish to maximize independence, autonomy, and control. Neither large sales nor large profits are deemed important beyond providing a sufficient and comfortable living for the entrepreneur. These folks don't want headaches, especially the kind that come with growth, employees, and ever-increasing capital requirements where assembling the resources is an ongoing task. They prefer a venture that can be handled on an intermittent basis.

Profit considerations play a more active role in Smaller Hi-Profit Ventures. To earn these profits, an entrepreneur will need to employ larger assets to build a good size restaurant, a small manufacturing operation, a regional accounting practice, etc. Partners and other managers are often needed to run a business that is clearly beyond the capabilities of a "solo operation." Some autonomy and control are given up, but not so much that the entrepreneur is forced to relinquish equity or ownership control and thus control over cash flow and profits, which are hoped to be substantial. Assembling resources and financing activities are fairly regular activities and can be particularly challenging since the lead entrepreneur may not have access to higher level financial talent.

Initially, sales are usually paramount in a High Growth Venture, but eventually profits are also expected to increase. The goal is to create a nationally or internationally known enterprise. Significant investment funds are generally required to start and operate this kind of venture. The bulk of investment funds tend to come either from large Private Placements, institutional sources in the form of venture capital, strategic partnerships with large organizations, or even an initial public offering prior to startup or shortly thereafter. The lead entrepreneur is willing to give up considerable autonomy, control, and independence due to a need to involve other team members, employees, venture capitalists, bankers, and others in order to realize the ultimate goal: the creation of a company with an extremely high market value so that a venture harvest, should one occur by selling part or all of the venture, will yield stratospheric returns to the original investors. Assembling the resources and financial activities for High Growth Ventures are continual, intense, and critical to the long-term success of the enterprise.

Both research and my experience have shown that the distinctions between Lifestyle, Smaller Hi-Profit, and High Growth Ventures are useful for entrepreneurial decision making. They are especially useful when estimating the time to create a venture, insuring personal and venture goal congruence, team member compatibility, and many other issues, including two which impinge directly on Entrepreneurial Finance. As we shall see in the next chapter, these venture categories are also useful when formulating feasible financial strategies and identifying relevant sources of financing.

Summary: How to Finance a New Venture

Entrepreneurial Finance is a subject concerned with the identification of viable financial strategies for new ventures, the development of these strategies using financial projections and budgeting techniques, and the implementation of a chosen financial strategy. An important distinction about Entrepreneurial Finance, in contrast to Corporate Finance, is that the actors involved in both financial analysis and decision making necessarily include the owners and initiators of the new venture. Effective entrepreneurs must know MORE than how to produce a new product or service and market it. They need to know how to finance a new venture.

And the latter requires a knowledge of Entrepreneurial Finance. It means possessing a knowledge of those particular numbers, measures, and concepts that relate specifically to the creation of new ventures. In terms of implementation, a knowledge of Entrepreneurial Finance means possessing a knowledge of how best to raise the funds needed for various kinds of new enterprises and the appropriate sources. However, as we shall now see, both of these activities, development of a financial strategy and its implementation, require owners to have a solid grasp of financial projections and budgets — a grasp they can only obtain by doing it themselves.

Endnotes

1 Accountants and others often refer to linked financial statements as "integrated financials."

2 The relationship between time and the pre-startup period and startup period is discussed in my book, *Entrepreneurship: Text, Cases, and Notes, op. cit.*, pp. 70-80.

3 These three venture categories and their overlap are examined in *Entrepreneurship: Text, Cases, and Notes, op. cit.*, pp. 74-77. Empirical work also shows that significant differences exist between practicing entrepreneurs "ex-entrepreneurs," and "serious nonstarters" in terms of these types of ventures. Serious nonstarters are people who made a demonstrated and significant effort to start a venture but never did so. "Ex-entrepreneurs" are people who started one or more ventures but eventually left entrepreneuring to work full time for someone else. Regarding serious nonstarters see my article "The Decision NOT To Become An Entrepreneur." *Frontiers Of Entrepreneurship Research 1983*, Center For Entrepreneurial Studies, Babson College, Wellesley, MA, 1983, pp. 206-207 which shows that 52% of the first ventures started by practicing entrepreneurs were Lifestyle Ventures or combination Lifestyle/Smaller High-Profit Ventures. By contrast 70% of the ventures *seriously considered* but not started by serious nonstarters were Smaller Profitable Ventures or High Growth Ventures. Ex-entrepreneurs were even higher (78%). See my "Ex-Entrepreneurs And The Decision To Start An Entrepreneurial Career," 1984, p. 452.

Raising Money For Your Venture

2

The Tie Between Financial Strategy, Sources of Funds, and Financial Projections

2

The Context

> *It was a pleasant spring afternoon when Trammel Crow came to class. We'd looked forward to his visit. His rags-to-riches rise as one the nation's top real estate developers was a fascinating story, and we looked forward to hearing it firsthand. As Mr. Crow entered our classroom, he brought some additional visitors with him, including several top Boston bankers. As the bankers sat down, Trammel Crow turned to them and remarked in a voice sufficiently loud enough for all the class to hear, "I'm sure glad you boys could make it to class today. Stick around. Maybe we'll do some business later … but I can't help wondering where all you fellows were years ago when I really needed you."*

Financial Objectives: Some Assumptions

We should all have Trammel Crow's dilemma. Instead, the vast majority of us find ourselves today where he was years ago when the bankers weren't, to say the least, terribly interested in his budding venture activities. Yet most of us would like to get where Trammel Crow was, financially speaking, on the day he visited our class.

At least, that is the assumption I'm going to make in this chapter. In fact, several assumptions must be made about any discussion of financial strategy since the latter is a very broad and often complex subject.

Specifically, I'm going to assume that, like Trammel Crow, you are "into entrepreneurship" for the long haul … that you are involved with entrepreneurship, whether you recognize it or not, as a career. This career may contain only one venture or, more likely, it will contain two or more new ventures. But whether one or many, your ultimate financial objective is to be pre-eminently bankable. Like Trammel Crow, you will want and need a track record that attracts people who are willing "to invest" (be it debt or equity) in just about anything you want to undertake … just because you are involved.

Your eventual needs may not be anywhere as great as Trammel Crow's. Perhaps they entail a modest expansion of your venture or sufficient funds to start another lifestyle or smaller hi-profit venture that requires more capital than you can afford to risk. Whichever the case, I am assuming you eventually want to create a reputation where potential investors or bankers will want "in" simply because you are involved. Ideally they won't even need a business plan (which does not mean you still shouldn't have one). They certainly won't need much explanation from you nor will they take much time to give you a decision. And, best of all, they will be quite happy with just a small piece of the action (if equity is involved) or willing to give you a very favorable interest rate and terms (if debt is involved).

Given this career objective, I also assume you will not be frivolous about using money ... whether your own savings or money borrowed from or invested by friends, relatives, or others willing to take a chance on you for economic or non-economic reasons. Given an awareness about relevant risks, I assume you will make rational, ethical, and economic decisions when using other peoples' money as if it were your own ... if not to maximize the return on stockholder's equity, then at least to maximize return on family harmony, friendship, or some other overarching goal.

Finally, I assume you recognize fully that others will want to know the value of your enterprise. This understanding means they will appraise your venture's track record in economic terms that may seem unfair, biased, incomplete, and possibly even unimportant to you. These people will include bankers, accountants, investors, and possibly even friends and relatives capable of taking a detached, hard look at your enterprise. Like it or not, I will assume they will force you to take a professional stance regarding your entrepreneurial activities, even when these activities include starting a Lifestyle Venture. In this light, such terms as return on equity, interest coverage, receivables turnover, and earnings valuation will be relevant to your venture pursuits.

Entrepreneurial Tasks and Multiple Rounds of Financing

The fundamental tasks of entrepreneurship are to find a customer opportunity, identify the customers, develop a product or service to satisfy their needs, and to assemble the resources required to make it happen. The sequence of these tasks can vary greatly, but often they are intertwined rather than sequential in any particular order. For instance, "assembling the resources" may be necessary not only to develop a product or service but also to find and verify a truly viable market opportunity.

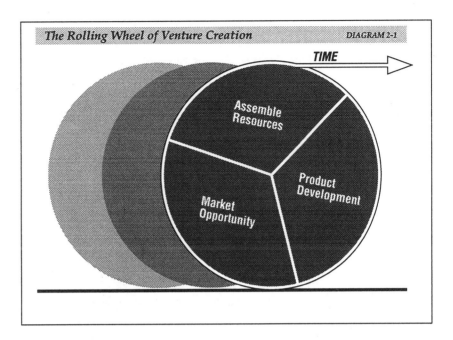

Furthermore, all three tasks require resources. Even "assembling the resources" requires resources of time, talent, and money. In today's world, it not only "takes money to make money," but it also "takes money to raise money." In fact, depending on the intended size of the new venture, both at startup and in terms of its growth, the task of assembling resources can be an awesome responsibility requiring considerable time, not to mention finders' fees.

Entrepreneurs, of course, have given us many creative examples of how to assemble resources, sometimes at little or no personal cost to the entrepreneur. The fine art of shifting financial risks to others is often a necessary task for entrepreneurs. But holding aside the issue of "who pays for the resources," we should not lose sight of a simple truth: "assembling the resources" is almost always no more than a euphemism for "raising money," even when the resource is not specifically money.

For instance, economists know that all resources have a cost. Sometimes it is hidden, but eventually it must be paid. For the entrepreneur, the payment may be in the form of equity; e.g., stock options given to employees who are willing to work for reduced salaries. Or perhaps it is a debt obligation the entrepreneur will have to pay in the future to a friendly supplier who is willing to take a risk that you will not walk away from your obligation.

Being good at raising money requires knowing precisely how much you have to raise and being able to raise it for the least cost. Achieving this goal means facing the reality that raising the money is often not a one time event.

Raising Money Is Not a One Time Event

This claim may seem obvious for High Growth Ventures. We know they usually go through several rounds of financing before reaching financial stability. But, after a little reflection, I believe you'll also see it applies to Small Hi-Profit Ventures and even most Lifestyle Ventures.

To help this process along, suppose you've decided to start a Lifestyle Venture. The venture will be something you've always wanted to do … after pursuing a lifetime hobby of collecting rare coins, you've decided to start a small newsletter business writing about the latest developments in rare coins. The time seems right. You can't stand your current job, and anyway it's just a matter of time before you'll have to find another. You know enough collectors to get started and, with a little luck, survive. You won't get rich, but there's no reason, with hard work plus running the venture from home, why you won't be able to replace your current salary in due time.

All this sounds like a classic "income substitution" venture. But let's peer just a short distance into the future to see the financial developments. The following chronology unfolds within 15 months.

> *Three months before startup, you calculate that you need $25,000 to cover living costs, equipment costs, some furniture, a second phone line (most of your current information is gathered by phone), and other startup expenses. You have $10,000 to invest. After some negotiating, you decide to accept an offer from a close friend for the remaining $15,000. In return, he gets 40% of the business. Even though you are investing less, you convince him that "your sweat" and other contributions are worth the difference.*
>
> *Six months after startup, the response to your newsletter has been very encouraging. However, the expense of running the business from your home has been higher than you anticipated. You are nearly breaking even but you aren't taking much of a salary yet. You need to lift subscriptions to eventually take a reasonable salary and start earning a profit. You need to inject some marketing money into the venture to make more people aware of your newsletter. You estimate that $15,000 will cover the cost of a direct marketing program. Your father knows your situation and offers to provide the funds. You agree, but only if he accepts a market interest rate. In your heart, however, you know that you'll pay him back every last penny even if you go under.*

Twelve months later the marketing efforts have paid off. You are earning a modest salary and paying interest on your debt. You haven't reduced the principal but a new development may make retiring the debt very possible. Your interaction with subscribers indicates they want more current information and are willing to pay for it. Instead of a monthly newsletter, a weekly could be very profitable. You already have the equipment; however, you'd have to hire two employees to produce a weekly and you'd have to get the business out of the house. Expenses would increase, but these would be offset by greater sales and margins. After estimating what you think the expansion will cost, you decide to approach your local banker for a $75,000 loan.

Three distinct financing decisions have been made during this short span of time. In effect, a Lifestyle Venture has gone through three rounds of financing. What's more, the likelihood seems high that additional financing rounds will occur as this venture shifts increasingly toward a Smaller Hi-Profit Venture —an occurrence that is relatively common for many lifestyle entrepreneurs who either experience more success than anticipated and/or decide, after all, that more enterprising venture goals are really their cup of tea. (See Diagram 2-2)

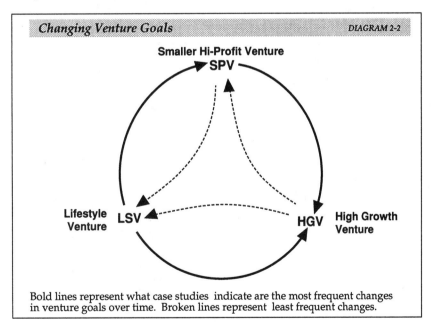

Changing Venture Goals   DIAGRAM 2-2

Smaller Hi-Profit Venture
SPV

Lifestyle Venture LSV

HGV High Growth Venture

Bold lines represent what case studies indicate are the most frequent changes in venture goals over time. Broken lines represent least frequent changes.

But let's concentrate on the past for a moment. Were the three financing decisions inevitable? Of course, we can debate the appropriateness of each decision. Other options might have been developed, however, given the level of information available to us at the time of each decision, it seems unlikely that THE NUMBER of decisions could have been reduced. After all, we didn't know what the market response would be. Nor did we know our customers would want a weekly newsletter. We could only discover these things by being in business.

In fact, a case could be made that the number of financing decisions could (and perhaps should) have been higher … at least by one if not more. This additional decision concerns the first $10,000 invested in the business — your $10,000. At issue is whether or not you could have given up less equity by spending all or some portion of your $10,000 before working your agreement with your friend for $15,000 and 40% of the business. As we shall now see, a better equity deal was probably available if the number of explicit financing decisions had been increased from three to four.

Assembling the Resources, Investor Returns, and the Entrepreneur's Tolerance for Uncertainty

There is a straightforward explanation why multiple rounds of financing should be the norm rather than the exception. The reason Entrepreneurial Finance should be a multiple event is that the risk level and likelihood of a venture failure often declines DURING THE PRE-STARTUP PERIOD as you move successfully from no more than an idea to actually opening for business. And, as risks decline during pre-startup, so do the returns available to investors.

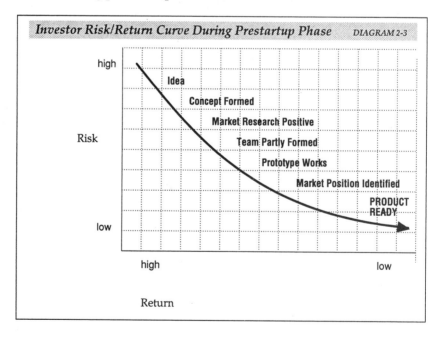

Investor Risk/Return Curve During Prestartup Phase   DIAGRAM 2-3

Idea
Concept Formed
Market Research Positive
Team Partly Formed
Prototype Works
Market Position Identified
PRODUCT READY

Risk — high / low
Return — high / low

Investor risk and return normally decline as one moves successfully through the pre-startup period

Of course, the investor risk-return curve does not always move downward. Unforeseen events may result in a new curve because you discover significant barriers or potential fatal flaws about your potential market, your product, or team members. As you discover these problems, you may be forced to abandon the venture or start down a new risk-return curve. Also, the risk-return position of your venture can quickly shift once you enter the Startup Period. For example, when you open for business suppose you discover the real acceptance of your product, the actual size of the market, and your capability to produce the product are significantly less than you expected. Investor risk increases dramatically under these conditions, and so does the return they require. To provide them with the higher return they now need, you will have to give them a greater share of equity in your venture.

Given these qualifications, it is important to understand why the investor's risk-return curve declines over time during the Pre-Startup Period. Let's take an extreme example to illustrate this point. I have an idea for a new airline company ... not exactly a Lifestyle Venture or even your run-of-the-mill High Growth Company because the pre-startup investment is huge. Nevertheless, I've got great experience in the industry and you believe that if anyone can pull it off, it's me. Although I have a little money, it's hardly sufficient to get to first base which is a detailed marketing and feasibility study. Fortunately you have $100,000 to invest — enough to get us to first base (or out of the game should the feasibility study show the venture infeasible). What percentage of the company would you want for your $100,000 at this point?

Now assume I have moved through the Pre-Startup Period, and I am about to see the first passengers fly on our planes. It hasn't been easy but it looks like it will actually happen. In fact, it has taken over two years to get to this point. I've already raised many millions to get this far. You aren't the first investor. More likely the 101st. Now how much would you want for your $100,000?

Of course, whatever number you would accept now, it should be considerably less than what you would have required two years ago when you would have been the first investor. My ability to move successfully through the pre-startup period — to assemble some resources (the people, the equipment, etc.) to better define the market opportunity, to develop the type and level of service — all these and other accomplishments have reduced both the uncertainty and the risk of the venture.

While this example is extreme, (few of us will start airline ventures), it also applies to ventures of smaller scale. We may be able to raise all the money we need to start a smaller venture right at the beginning, just as we did with our newsletter venture. But it is not necessarily the best time to raise everything we need. The price we will have to pay may be too high, and certainly will be higher than if we raised only what we need to move down the risk curve.

High Risk Requires High Returns & More Equity for Investors

For example, our airline example applies directly to our rare coin newsletter business. We didn't need to raise all $25,000 prior to starting our newsletter. We had $10,000 in savings which could have been used to get closer to startup or perhaps even into startup by renting or borrowing equipment for the first issue. Such action does entail greater risk for us. It tests our tolerance to live with uncertainty … and the uncertainty about where the next round of funds will come from is one of the most difficult to tolerate. Yet it separates, in my view, the excellent entrepreneurs from the pack because, as we shall see in a moment, it allows them to make the best financing deals while running a lean operation that is neither overcapitalized nor undercapitalized.

Developing Your Financial Strategy

The declining relationship during the Pre-Startup Period (and possibly the Startup Period) between risk, investor returns, and time argues for using your own money and retaining all the equity until the venture increases in value.

That's the theory. Reality, however, has a way of complicating the best of theories. Several complications can emerge. For example, you may find it financially imprudent to invest all the funds you have in order to move down the risk curve and reach a new valuation plateau. Or the funds you have to invest simply aren't sufficient to get you to a new plateau. Or you may be without financial resources right from the beginning. Or you may be wedded firmly to the notion that you never use your own money for venture startups. Or you may come face-to-face with the "bird in the hand" dilemma when, early in the life of a venture, an "angel" appears who will immediately put up all the money you need into the foreseeable future for, of course, a sizeable slice of the venture. Inevitably, the question surfaces: What if I take only what I need now, giving up a smaller amount of equity, and then can't raise more money later?

I've faced each of these dilemmas as an entrepreneur. None are easy to resolve. But resolution is possible if you have a strong command of the numbers, an understanding of what you are getting versus giving up, a solid grasp of your VENTURE goals, the likelihood of whether these venture goals will change, and your tolerance for uncertainty (i.e., your faith in the venture, and your faith in your ability to raise funds in the future). What is critical is to obtain the proper amount of funds for the financial strategy ultimately selected. Here the concept of "threshold capitalization" is crucial since it lies at the heart of successfully gathering resources. Let us examine this concept, for an understanding of it reveals why the selection of a viable financial strategy and its execution require the development of good financial projections.

The Goal of Financial Strategy: Threshold Capitalization

The term "threshold capitalization" refers to the amount of capital needed to achieve a critical startup milestone, one that will result in a significantly higher valuation for your venture by others when they are loaning you capital or investing it. Threshold capitalization means being neither undercapitalized nor overcapitalized as one moves toward the next round of financing. Both are a problem. Undercapitalization is appreciated more widely by today's entrepreneurs and its consequences are evident. You either go out of business or raise additional capital, usually at unfavorable terms because you didn't have sufficient funds to finance the venture in the first place.

The perils of overcapitalization are less appreciated but can be just as serious. The kneejerk reaction of "raising all the money I can get" to avoid being undercapitalized often leads to loss of control, a decline in creativity, and a tempting environment for theft, embezzlement, and a financial sandpit conducive to soft living. Even if the living isn't soft, too much capital often causes team members, employees, and others associated with a venture to lose their intensity. And as most experienced entrepreneurs will tell you, a hungry intensity, a willingness to burn the midnight oil when necessary, makes all the difference between venture success and failure.

Determining the threshold capitalization for your venture was a tedious if not impossible job before the personal computer and Ronstadt's FINANCIALS made it feasible. But for the moment, let's pretend you know the right amount of resources you need to assemble. There are still some other issues to resolve regarding the development of your financial strategy.

OPM Versus EMO Strategies

Within this context, we come to a critical departure point that shapes your future financial strategy: Whose money will you use ... your own ... or others? Some entrepreneurs live and breathe the doctrine of OPM (Other Peoples Money ... rather than risk my own money). Others are just as extreme in their allegiance to EMO (Entrepreneur's Money Only ... and no one else's money in the venture).

Both strategies are possible in certain situations. But both are usually inefficient and not viable for most ventures. Like buying real estate with "nothing down," starting a venture solely with other people's money is much less feasible in the real world of entrepreneuring than you might expect.

The likelihood of exclusive OPM also dwindles as the scope of your venture increases. As your venture becomes more enterprising in its sales goals, asset needs usually increase and so does the need to deal with investors who are neither friends or relatives. Very few of these investors will be interested in any venture where the lead entrepreneur does not also have a substantial dollar commitment in the venture. The dollar amount may not be large in absolute terms, but it still is "substantial" as a percentage of the entrepreneur's net worth.

Also, exclusive OPM can backfire. The old refrain is very true about "the golden rule of financing is: he who has the gold also rules." Other peoples money also means "other people" messing with your venture. It can mean loss of majority control either at the time of investment or almost certainly later if you do not meet expectations and/or legal agreements. At the very least, OPM has a price. It means spending valuable time keeping others informed about the progress (or lack of it) of your venture. Whether your financial partner is a relative, the bank, a private investor, or a professional venture capitalist, you will do your share of reporting, convincing, and negotiating about the past, present, and future course of your venture.

The same kinds of comments can be said of EMO. Unless you are fabulously wealthy or the venture has little or no capital needs, you will soon find yourself seeking "other people's" money. In either instance, a good argument can still be made to use some funds from other sources as a validity test of the venture's concept and your ideas about implementation. This use of OPM increases as the scope of the venture increases, as Diagram 2-4 illustrates.

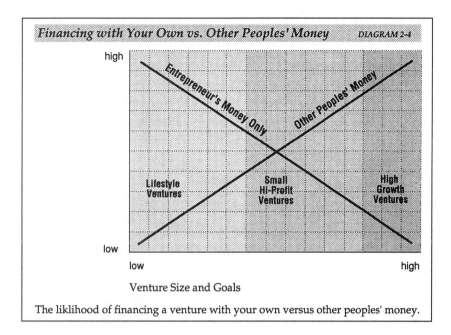

Financing with Your Own vs. Other Peoples' Money   DIAGRAM 2-4

high

Entrepreneur's Money Only

Other Peoples' Money

Lifestyle Ventures

Small Hi-Profit Ventures

High Growth Ventures

low

low   high

Venture Size and Goals

The liklihood of financing a venture with your own versus other peoples' money.

Ownership: How Much Is Needed?

If exclusive OPM or EMO are usually infeasible and/or not recommended, then what is left? The answer is a combination whereby the lead entrepreneur does or does not have majority ownership. You will probably need OPM. You will also probably have to invest some money of your own to attract investment funds from other folks.

This situation means you must decide very early in the life of your venture how much equity you are willing to give up. One goal you should have is majority ownership and/or majority control through the startup period. Only under rare circumstances and conditions should you give up majority control during the pre-startup or startup periods of your venture. There are too many instances of ventures that have gone awry when the lead entrepreneur cannot call the shots in a timely and flexible way, or simply no longer has the incentive to stick with the venture through tough times. The incentive "to walk" away from the venture becomes too great.

Moreover, the political dynamics of putting a new organization together demand a clear statement of who is "in command," who has the control and power to call the shots. The pre-startup and early startup period are no time for the kind of office political warfare that permeates larger organizations. However, your position will be clouded by lack of majority control during a time of great flux and uncertainty. The realities of startup are that it is simply too easy for someone to undermine your position since a fair amount of "second guessing" is possible.

Bootstrap Strategies Versus Deep Pocket-Fast Burn Strategies

One area susceptible to second guessing is a strategic decision you
will make about the level of financial resources to commit to your
enterprise. There are many ways to start a new venture that result in
a successful outcome for the entrepreneur(s) and investor(s). What
is unfortunate is that many fledgling entrepreneurs fail to consider
these options but lock into "the way" very early during the conception of the venture.

Along the financial dimension, two extreme choices exist regarding the initial size and rate of growth of a new venture. These
choices are represented by two contrasting approaches to venture
financing: bootstrap versus deep pocket-fast burn strategies.

The essence of these strategies is understood by asking two questions: Are you going to spend as little money as possible to launch
your venture and get into business as soon as possible to see if a
market really exists for your product? Or do competitive or other circumstances require you to spend heavily on product and marketing
development, as well as other fixed operating and marketing expenses before you get into the market, or at the time of product launch?

Bootstrap strategies refer to situations where you spend the least
possible (and are still not undercapitalized). It is often a strategy
where you try to minimize total equity investment prior to product
launch and then when the true conditions of market demand reveal
themselves (and risk and uncertainty are reduced), you leverage the
investment using debt in order to maximize your return on equity.

Deep pocket-fast burn strategies are just the opposite. They assume the need for a much faster product roll out. Greater resources
are needed and "burned" because it may be the only way to reach a
new or diffuse market. Without a large critical mass of resources,
you will not be able to produce a product with enough competitive
features, or you will not be able to make the investment needed
in marketing research, market positioning, and market
communications.

The choice between these polar strategies isn't always clear cut.
Both may work under certain modified conditions. It may also be
advantageous and/or necessary to modify one of these strategies.
For instance, you may believe a deep pocket approach is most appropriate but, upon running your financials you discover that your
pockets (and your investors) just aren't deep enough. The comparable exercise for a bootstrap strategy may reveal that a zero
marketing budget (strict word-of-mouth approach) simply won't
work. But determining precisely what you can afford to spend will
send you back to your projections.

After "How Much" and "When" comes "What Kind of Money?"

A traditional way of thinking about financial strategy for startups has been to distinguish between the type of investment funds used. Are they debt funds or equity funds? (See box for definitions.)

Some Quick Definitions

Debt Funds are monies that require a payment of interest on a regular basis (usually monthly, quarterly, or annually) or else the IRS will consider them equity funds. This interest on the debt represents a cash outflow of monies at a time in the life of the venture when it is usually paramount to conserve as much cash as possible and utilize cash for operating purposes, particularly product development and marketing needs. The upside of debt from the entrepreneur's perspective is that the return is fixed and no equity ownership is given up to those providing the funds. The downside is that the venture and/or the entrepreneur may be liable for the repayment of the loan even if the venture fails.

Equity Funds are monies that you or other investors provide solely for the purpose of ultimately earning some return on your investment in the future. They do not expect to earn interest on their money while you are building your venture. Rather they hope to share in the appreciation of the assets put to work for you. However, their return can be unlimited (in most cases). These equity investors may lose all their money or they may earn an uncapped return. They've said, unlike the debt investor, "I'll forego the sure 12% on my money for the opportunity to receive my prorata share of the profits and, in case of a sale of stock, the appreciation in the venture's value to others at the time of the sale."

The distinction between debt and equity is useful because these two terms impact quite differently on both cash flow and the ultimate return an investor will receive. However, it is not entirely valid nor sufficient to think about financial strategy solely in terms of debt-equity combinations. Debt or equity tell us the FORM of the capital we need and we can compare their costs relative to one another. But they don't answer the two fundamental questions of Entrepreneurial Finance which shape financial strategy for new venture creation: namely, How much money do we need to make a substantial increase in the valuation of the enterprise ... so that the next round of financing will be still cheaper? And when do we need this money? Once these questions are answered, it becomes very appropriate to ask: What form should the money take? ... since the answer will influence the response to the fourth basic question of Entrepreneurial Finance: Where should we look to raise the needed funds?

Debt Versus Equity: Which Is Better?

A debate has raged, and continues today, among entrepreneurs about which is better to use — debt or equity. Both have their

advocates. And, like most matters of divided opinion, the right
answer is "It all depends."

It depends on the kind of venture you are starting, your track
record, your comfort zone or risk preference, as well as your access
to debt funds versus equity funds and the terms associated with
each.

For instance, there are ventures where debt should be avoided or
minimized because both the risk and financial requirements are so
large (relative to your net worth) that a catastrophic loss means personal financial disaster for you and your family. No one should
jump out a window because of a venture failure. As a rule of thumb,
it is generally wise to use equity funds during the pre-startup period
even if debt is available. The exceptions are when the funds will be
used to purchase fixed assets whose resale value under liquidation
conditions will still be sufficient to cover the debt; or when the debt
is effectively working capital because you have immediate and assured access to the product or service to be delivered and you have
pre-paid or otherwise guaranteed customers (i.e., the real risk of the
venture is very low).

If equity funds are not available, the prudent course is to look for
another venture where the financial barriers are not so high. Also, if
you or others are not prepared to risk equity funds, then perhaps
something is wrong with the venture.

Sources of Funds to Implement Your Financial Strategy

Answers to the three questions we've discussed — how much,
when, and what form (debt or equity) — often determines WHERE
to look for the money we need for a new venture or to expand an existing venture.

Where, When, What Form, and How Much

Your source of funds is determined greatly by how much you need
and when you need the money (during the pre-startup or startup
periods, or later), and whether you require debt versus equity funds.

Sources During Pre-Startup

The most important sources for the vast majority of entrepreneurs
during the pre-startup period are personal and informal sources and
supplier financing. In almost every instance, early seed money
(whether debt or equity) for most ventures comes from:

- your own savings
- friends or relatives
- informal investors

These three sources are ordered generally in terms of the magnitude of the financial need — from low to high. For instance, ventures that require small amounts of startup capital can be handled exclusively from savings. But as the startup amounts increase, we find ourselves reaching out to relatives, acquaintances, and ultimately "informal investors" for larger chunks of seed money. This latter group is extremely important since they fund a great many ventures. They are called "informal" because they have no organizational representation. You can't find them in the "yellow pages" of your phone book, as you can professional venture capitalists, Small Business Investment Companies [SBICs], underwriters, and other investment companies. You need to know someone who knows someone who knows an informal investor. Generally what you will find is a person who has the financial means, desire, and sophistication to invest in your venture.

Sources During Startup

Once the business has opened its doors, most investment funds come from bank loan officers and supplier credits. Bankers, venture capitalists, and other institutional sources rarely invest before a venture is operating for some time and possesses a defensible case for expansion money.

How quickly you need to raise funds can also affect the source you seek to tap.

Necessary Sources and Times

Source	Average Time Needed
you and your family	usually an immediate response
relatives and friends	2 to 4 weeks
local bank	2 to 4 weeks
informal investors	1 to 3 months
venture capitalists	3 to 6 months

The choice of financial strategy often indicates the source of possible funds. Of course, sometimes the reverse is true. Because of personal contacts and reputation, a source of funds may be readily available and influence the financial strategy of a venture. The source may be a parent or rich relative (Uncle Albert) who wants to see you in business or a professional venture capitalist beating a path to your door. In either case, the kind of venture and financial strategy you pursue will reflect the interests, aspirations, and financial capacity of good old Uncle Albert or Galactic Venture Capital, Ltd. These interests will be quite different, unless of course Uncle Albert happens to be the senior partner at Galactic.

Letting the source of funds dictate financial strategy may sound a little like putting the cart before the horse. Actually it may be less important than it seems given the multitude of ways that usually exist to realize a successful venture, assuming there is not a major mismatch in goals.

Using Ronstadt's FINANCIALS to Set Financial Strategy and Implement It

Ronstadt's FINANCIALS is an invaluable tool to help you determine the first two fundamental questions that shape financial strategy: How much money do you need and when do you need it? Ronstadt's FINANCIALS is also designed to help you estimate the actual time (hence cash) it will take to start the venture. You can also use the program to determine the amount of debt and/or equity you should use; and the likely valuation of your venture by bankers or investors.

Using Ronstadt's FINANCIALS to Estimate Time Factors

Along with estimating sales, estimating the time it will actually take to launch a venture is subject to considerable error. In fact, a "rule of thumb" has emerged over the years which, itself, reveals the magnitude of the problem. This guideline states that "whatever time you think it will take you to start a new venture, triple it." Now, if we think for a moment, this guideline is telling us that on average a new venture startup is subject to a 300% error regarding the estimate of the pre-startup period. I don't doubt it, but shouldn't we be able to do better than a 300% error with some serious planning? In fact, such planning is mandatory when one considers the usual consequences on capitalization of a 300% error in estimating the startup date. It's likely that a fair share of the undercapitalized ventures that are started can trace their lack of sufficient funds to the 300% delay in earning operating income while pre-startup expenses continued to mount.

Ronstadt's FINANCIALS helps you to better estimate time in three ways. First, it makes planning in small time units (months, weeks, or even days) considerably simpler than was heretofore possible. Why is planning in small units good? It forces you to be explicit, realistic, and more accurate about what you can achieve.

Second, you can easily shift your estimates as soon as planning and actual events prove that your original time estimate can't be met. In the past people might actually have known after a certain point that their original projections were no longer on target regarding the startup date. It was just too hard to change them.

Third, you can tie detailed budgets into your financial projection. As the budgets are changed or updated to better reflect reality, your financial projections are altered automatically.

Using Ronstadt's FINANCIALS to Determine the Debt Versus Equity Question

You can use Ronstadt's FINANCIALS to see the impact of debt on the Balance Sheet, Cash Flow Statement, and Key Measures in terms of the Debt-Equity Ratio. How to do this is explained later, however, all you need to do is simply change the interest rate and see the impact on the P&L and Cash Flow Statement.

Summary: Projections and Educated Entrepreneurs

The sages of old tell us that life is a question of balance. Entrepreneurial life is no different. The financial job of the lead entrepreneur (not just whoever is in charge of finance and accounting) is to be certain that the right amount of money is being used to start and operate a new venture … neither too little nor too much. Otherwise the venture will be off-balance and in danger of falling off course.

If the objective of any financial strategy is to minimize costs while maximizing the returns to an entrepreneur, then the questions of how much is needed and when it is needed are vital and non-trivial questions. Both questions are interrelated and depend on the lead entrepreneur knowing when the accomplishments of certain milestones during the pre-startup period will cause a significant increase in the valuation of the venture to potential investors.

Can people come up with a good financial strategy plus do a good job of executing it without a good set of financial projections? Of course they can. There are many examples of successful ventures where entrepreneurs have operated by the seat of their pants. Some people have an intuitive feel for such things. Others are simply lucky.

But good entrepreneuring should never be left solely to luck and intuition. The most successful entrepreneurs I know, those with several ventures under their belts and/or several decades of experience, do NOT rely on luck or intuition. They have seen their share of good luck and bad luck. They also make intuitive decisions when they've exhausted the rational sources of inquiry that are available to them. But they rarely go on "gut instinct" alone.

Gut instinct about the amount and timing of investment funds seldom suffices. The decisions involved are too complicated. Thus far our discussion shows that "assembling resources" is not a one-time decision. The best course often calls for multiple efforts of fund raising, whether the funds be debt or equity. Key milestones have to be identified and financial projections should be generated at the completion of each milestone. These projections should reveal the amount of capital you need to reach the next milestone while providing a basis for greater valuations of your venture.

Over the last few years a number of articles have been written about "the new entrepreneurs." Sometimes the "new" refers to high tech entrepreneurs, or women entrepreneurs, or minority entrepreneurs, or corporate entrepreneurs. But there is fundamentally nothing new about these entrepreneurs. They have always been there, albeit in varying degrees. The only "new" entrepreneurs that exist today that didn't 100 or 1000 years ago are the "educated entrepreneurs."

Unlike the entrepreneurs of yesteryear, a growing cadre of entrepreneurs is gaining experience after having been formally educated in the field of Entrepreneurial Studies or, at least, having educated themselves about entrepreneurship. The notion that entrepreneurship is something that can be learned only via experience is crumbling. A new revolutionary notion is being institutionalized in literally thousands of college classrooms. This idea holds that entrepreneurship is a body of knowledge about the creation of enterprises that can be taught and learned. Its premise is that those who have a better understanding of entrepreneurship will do better than they would have without their instruction.

Only time will tell if this premise is valid, however, there is already some evidence to support it. For instance, it appears that entrepreneurial longevity and long-term success is linked strongly to proper planning and preparation, both for the career in general and the specific venture in question. One of the lessons educated entrepreneurs will carry with them is the need to use financial projections and budgets to make better choices about financial strategy and sources of financing, whether the venture is their first or twenty-first.

The Value of Financial Projections

3

And Why Spreadsheets Don't Do the Job

3

The Fatal Limitations of Spreadsheets

The horror stories recounted in Chapter One convey three messages:

- Doing nothing or ignoring the needs of entrepreneurial finance isn't the answer.
- Manual calculation certainly is not the answer. Such drudgery represents a leap back to the Dark Ages of Entrepreneurial Finance.
- The conventional spreadsheet is not the answer. While spreadsheets are invaluable for many kinds of calculating needs, they simply fail to generate the kind of quick financial information that people need to make intelligent decisions about creating new ventures.

In fact, very few people can generate complete sets of linked financial statements. Even trained analysts find the process difficult at best. Often even they make mistakes. Today the process is viable if you are a highly skilled financial or accounting analyst plus a spreadsheet power user. 1

||||||||||||||| NOTE *The best discussion of spreadsheet errors I've seen was just published by Mark Chussil, "Computer-Based Planning: A PC Survival Guide," The Journal Of Business Strategy, January/February, 1988, pp. 38-42.*

But even if you can generate a complete set of interrelated financial statements, it is impossible to compare different scenarios in a meaningful way using conventional spreadsheets. It is also next to impossible to:

- generate detailed budgets that feed into your financial projections
- view monthly data on a quarterly or yearly basis
- quickly alter the starting date for your projections due to time delays
- quickly convert financial data to percentages, breakevens, and other key measures

At the same time, programs that work in tandem with spreadsheets by producing a financial model or "template" don't deliver the results. This opinion is not just mine but the voice of the marketplace. The market has spoken about templates in a very clear and definitive way. Only a few thousand have been sold. 2 No one, except the vendors themselves, touts templates as a solution for the vast majority of existing and potential users. The reasons why templates have failed are because they are:

- too slow
- too inflexible
- too hard to learn

Overall, using a template with a conventional spreadsheet is just too hard and takes too much time to produce meaningful financial projections and budgets. Templates simply require too much knowledge of sophisticated programming techniques ("macros") to make them flexible and practical for the average user. You have to be a power user *before you can* take practical advantage of a template ... and even then there are fatal limitations.

What Good Proforma Financials and Budgets Tell You about an Uncertain World

Despite all the difficulties with existing tools, good proformas are necessary. They are needed to help us answer questions about a variety of opportunities and problems we encounter in our professional and personal lives. They are not just a business tool. Proformas are useful to chart the future for any kind of venture ... whether it be a business, a nonprofit enterprise, a new government program, or even a personal venture. [3]

Proformas let us answer key questions about:
- How feasible is the venture?
- What amount of resources will be needed?
- What policies and plans can we pursue given these resources?

In short, financial projections are the heart of financial strategy. And, like it or not, financial strategy usually has a monumental impact on ultimate venture success. Shaping your financial strategy is a learning process and financial projections are an important mechanism to help you learn about your financial strategy. In fact, financial projections are used to help you improve your financial strategy by forcing you to be explicit. You need to be explicit, especially when the temptation is great to be vague and casual about decisions that can have momentous impact on our lives and often the lives of others.

Over the years, my work with entrepreneurs has revealed several other practical reasons why you need an easy yet sophisticated tool for generating financial statements and budgets. For instance:
- Good projections help you to determine if you should start or pursue some venture. They also give you the confidence to assume risks, including personal loan guarantees, second mortgages, and other obligations you will probably have to assume when you start a new venture.

- Good projections help to improve your odds of starting. People often talk about venture failure rates, but they forget about the many ventures that are seriously considered but never started. Good projections can help to reduce uncertainty and provide a sense of confidence that encourages people to start what should be started.
- Good projections help you to avoid mistakes. Even rough or preliminary proformas can sometimes help you to avoid spending needless hours on something that can never work out.

Then there is reality. Even if you don't "buy into" these very legitimate reasons for producing projections, there is one other reason you cannot afford to ignore. Investors, loan officers, and others demand them ... not because they are irrational folks who like to see entrepreneurs work, but for the reasons just cited.

> *"When Ben Cohen and Jerry Greenfield sat down to write a business plan for the ice cream parlor they wanted to open in Vermont, they knew that they too needed a forecast, or rather, that the Small Business Administration wouldn't give them a loan guarantee without seeing some numbers."* [4]

Valid Objections to Financial Projections

We need to ask: Why don't more people develop financial projections and prepare detailed budgets and schedules if they are so necessary? There have been some very valid reasons up to this point for avoiding the task.

1 **They are too hard to do.**
No argument here. I hated to do them. I even hated asking my students to produce them.

2 **They become obsolete too quickly.**
Obsolescence depends on the nature of the venture, but there is no doubt that, for some ventures, industry and market circumstances can change so quickly and frequently that their projections require continual work that is simply too time-consuming. The experience of Sun Microsystems seems to reflect this situation.

> *"You don't need a plan for a hundred-person company,' says Scott McNealy, Chief Executive Officer of Sun Microsystems, in Mountain View, California, ... "The key," he says, "is knowing in your gut' what cash flow is like, how expenses are running in relation to sales." In a startup, things change too quickly for any plan. "You basically throw out all assumptions every three weeks," he says.*
>
> *"The plan forecasts sales of $4 million in the first year, fiscal 1983, and $10 million in the second. The venture capitalists felt that was wildly optimistic," says McNealy.*
>
> *"So the fact that we came in at $9 million and $39 million obsoleted this thing so fast, there was never any reason to go back to it.*
>
> *Last year, Sun's net income rose 40%, to $12 million on sales of $210 million. Goals only limit you," McNealy says.*
>
> *"Setting down expectations would only have slowed us down."* [5]

3   **Unforeseen events will occur that will invalidate them.**
    Disraeli put it so nicely: "What happens most often is least expected. What is most expected, rarely occurs."

4   **They are not reliable.**
    Why? The GIGO Rule (Garbage In, Garbage Out) dominates the process. Furthermore, the garbage can be:

- bad assumptions
- forgotten or hidden assumptions
- bad arithmetic
- incorrect formulas
- incorrect cell references and other typical spreadsheet errors
- faulty accounting procedures

I believe Burgess Jamieson, General Partner in Sigma Partners, a Silicon Valley venture capital firm, sums it up best. He calls spreadsheets "a disaster for business-plan quality." "By using the program," he says, "entrepreneurs can crank out all sorts of great-looking sets of numbers without any personal commitment to them." 6

How the Software Program "Ronstadt's FINANCIALS" Overcomes these Objections

Ronstadt's FINANCIALS has been designed by experts to help reduce, if not eliminate, many of the objections to developing and using financial projections. Let's see how it actually addresses these complaints.

The Difficulty Objection

The things that are difficult about projections, and require great expertise emanate from two distinct sources: difficulty using the computer and software and difficulty with finance and accounting. Ronstadt's FINANCIALS limits what you have to know (more importantly, what you have to "remember") about both.

The Obsolescence and Uncertainty Objection

Ronstadt's FINANCIALS takes a matter of minutes to make substantial changes in a set of financial projections. In fact, entire new scenarios can be developed in a matter of seconds, whereas major changes using traditional spreadsheets require days, often weeks, of work by experienced analysts.

Ronstadt's FINANCIALS is not a crystal ball that lets you predict the future with exact precision. The odds are still overwhelming that the reality your venture experiences will not be what you forecasted in your financials. But Ronstadt's FINANCIALS allows you to react faster, and to see what unforeseen events mean to your business as they occur.

The Garbage Can Be Bad Arithmetic

The math is automatic. You don't have to worry about "ranges" being properly defined when you need to have a column of numbers added up.

The Garbage Can Be Incorrect or Unintelligible Formulas

The formulas used in Ronstadt's FINANCIALS are written in English. Also, the formulas are expressed as close to normal English sentences as possible. Finally, they have been written by experts and reviewed by experts in finance and accounting who are familiar with the industry or area in question.

The Garbage Can Be Incorrect Cell References and Other Typical Spreadsheet Errors

Ronstadt's Financials is not cell-based. It is NOT a spreadsheet, but a "rowsheet." Its formulas are written for each row. The downside implication is that Ronstadt's FINANCIALS is not as flexible as a cell-based spreadsheet. The upside is that Ronstadt's FINANCIALS is subject to far fewer errors that can be fatal to producing an accurate set of financial statements than cell-based spreadsheets.

The Garbage Can Be Faulty Interpretation of Accounting and Financial Data

Accounting is neither a simple nor static subject. It has a very precise way of doing things. It also has a group of professionals who define what is kosher according to "commonly accepted principles of accounting." While Ronstadt's FINANCIALS is NOT an accounting program, it does use accepted accounting prin-

ciples to generate and organize its financial projections and
budgets. It also provides you with extensive "help" regarding
finance and accounting terminology so you will be less likely to
make an interpretative error.

The Reliability Objection

The Garbage Can Be Bad Assumptions

Ronstadt's FINANCIALS forces you to think explicitly about your
assumptions by locating them together in a single statement. In
fact, the assumptions are so important, we've given them their
own statement, the Assumptions Statement. Also, the program
executes so quickly compared to others in terms of producing
finished sets of financials that you have more time to think about
your assumptions and try various scenarios using different
assumptions.

The Garbage Can Be Forgotten or Hidden Assumptions

The major assumptions for the pre-defined sets of financial statements are already identified for you by Ronstadt's FINANCIALS.
Of course, you can change these assumptions, add new ones, or
delete existing ones. The critical point is that Ronstadt's FINAN-
CIALS possesses a defined area where assumptions are made so it
is nearly impossible to ignore or hide your assumptions. Remember, all projections have assumptions and now the microcomputer gives us the opportunity to be much more explicit and
better organized about making and displaying these assumptions. Unfortunately, the assumptions imbedded in detailed, real
world financial projections produced by spreadsheet programs
usually are dispersed or hidden from view. They can be con-
centrated, but gathering them in one location takes considerable
time and expertise. By contrast, Ronstadt's FINANCIALS allows
you to concentrate on your venture and its underlying assumptions ... not on becoming a computer jockey.

Summary: What's Needed for Superior Venture Thinking

The real need of entrepreneurs is not just a set of financial statements. The real need is a capability to think critically about a variety of venture scenarios — where each scenario represents a unique set of assumptions and, consequently, a unique set of financial projections about an existing venture or a proposed venture concept.

The truth of the matter is that spreadsheets and templates don't allow or facilitate the generation of venture scenarios by and for entrepreneurs. As such, they inhibit superior venture thinking. What spreadsheets do is empower financial analysts, especially those employed in larger organizations, since they are the only ones who understand how a particular set of projections works after spending months putting them together. What has been created is a cadre of spreadsheet gurus who, at $50,000 to $80,000 per year, are the high-priced equivalent (for the computer generation) of yesterday's high-priced, "indispensable" secretary whose unique filing system is only understood by its originator.

Larger organizations can operate with this overhead, or at least they can survive. But entrepreneurs running new and smaller ventures cannot afford the luxury. They need to develop and compare different venture scenarios. They need to test and retest their assumptions as new information becomes available about alternative courses of action. Only one tool, Ronstadt's FINANCIALS, answers this need.

Endnotes

1   I want to emphasize that I'm not talking about a simple spreadsheet (say 20 or 30 rows by 20 columns) for a single statement, e.g., an Income Statement. Unfortunately, individual financial statements have very limited value for projection purposes. To have value, Income Statements need to be linked to Balance Sheets, Cash Flow Statements, as well as other statements. Here we are talking about spreadsheets that vary in size from 800 to 2000 rows and 30 columns. The last set of financial projections I did using a spreadsheet program was approximately 1200 rows by 30 columns. That means 36,000 cells that had to be defined. Assuming 40% were blank or empty space, that still means over 20,000 cells had to be referenced with a formula. The opportunity for error is immense and trying to check formulas that look like: @ SUM (B23. = $54) / (C273) * 1.20 is next to impossible. The real horror is that these errors generally go undetected. Franklynn Peterson and Judi K. Turkel who write a column called the *Business Computer* state: "We've found minor errors in three out of four self-written spreadsheets we've seen companies using, and major blunders in one out of four."

2   Actually, the largest number of templates sold by a single company were the very first templates ever produced for VisiCalc in the early 1980s. Since then the market has gradually discovered that templates don't work because as soon as you need to change their format you have to contend with formulas that are meaningful only to experienced programmers.

3   The need for "financial foresight" is explained in the context of entrepreneurial management by Peter Drucker. See his *Innovation And Entrepreneurship*, Harper & Row, New York,1985, p. 189 and pp. 193-197.

4   See Erik Larson's article "The Best-Laid Plans," *Inc. Magazine*, February, 1987, p. 62.

5   "Big Plans: Business Plans Aren't Getting Better, They're Getting Longer," *Inc. Magazine*, February, 1987, p. 84.

6   *Ibid*, p. 64.

Thinking About Your Venture's Assumption

4

4

A Framework for Financial Projections

Part of the confusion that surrounds the arcane subject of financial projections centers on the failure of existing conceptual frameworks to chart the forest without getting lost in the minutiae of accounting and finance. Existing frameworks may be sufficient for accountants and financial analysts, but they fall short for people who have no more than a passing knowledge of finance and accounting, yet need to create financial projections for entrepreneurial decision making.

A basic premise of this chapter is that most people do get lost when trying to develop financial projections. They end up wasting large chunks of time working with the numbers, and consequently do not spend sufficient time "thinking" about their venture and the underlying factors or assumptions that determine their venture's financial projections.

To help us avoid getting lost, I'm compelled to describe a slightly different approach to doing financial projections. This approach will assume three conditions that are crucial hallmarks, in my opinion, of the entrepreneurial environment surrounding venture creation and expansion:

1 *Numerous ways exist to start a new venture or expand an existing one and the first venture concepts identified by entrepreneurs are seldom the best ones.* Each concept requires entrepreneurs to make one or more creative assumptions about how the venture will acquire its products, its customers, and how it will organize and operate to produce and market its goods and services. But each venture concept can have a very different impact on the level of initial capital and ongoing financial requirements, as well as the eventual financial return realized by the venture.

To consider many venture concepts, and to identify the better ones, entrepreneurs must develop an expertise in assumption making. At the very least, they must become "comfortable" making assumptions. Each set of assumptions represents a unique way to create or expand a venture. The result for our framework is the creation of a separate and overarching statement, The *Assumptions Statement*. As we shall see, it drives the results produced by all other statements.

2 *Uncertainty is high for most entrepreneurial ventures but most often the critical uncertainty is the uncertainty of the actual market size for a proposed product or service.* This market uncertainty means that the accurate projection of product/service sales acquires an added importance for entrepreneurs, one where "the top line" takes on an equal, if not greater, importance than the bottom line. The result for our framework is a separate *Revenue Forecast Statement* that focuses exclusively on sales revenues.

3   *The ebb and flow of cash drop off over the short term often determines death or survival for entrepreneurial ventures.* The result for our framework is the inclusion of the *Cash Flow Statement* as a critical tool of planning. This statement, more than any other, helps to determine how much money we need to launch a venture. It also tells us if and when we need more funding after launching a new venture, and how much we will need to sustain it.

An Overview of the Basic Framework

There are four groups of statements that form the backbone of venture scenario planning. The four groups of statements are the:

- Assumptions Statement
- Core Financial Statements
- Supporting Statements
- Analytic Statements

Most of the statements we will discuss may be familiar turf to those readers with some accounting and finance background. However, the Assumptions Statement will be new to most readers. It is not usually referred to as a "statement." However, it is, in my opinion, the most important statement because it is the basis upon which all of your venture's financial projections are derived, as reflected in the Core Statements, Supporting Statements, and Analytic Statements. (See Diagram 4-1)

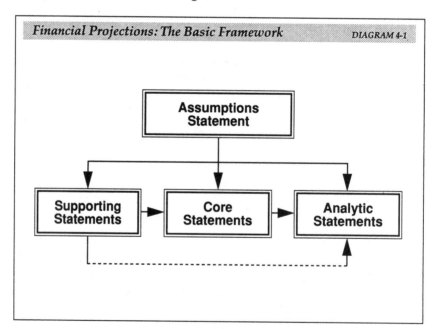

Financial Projections: The Basic Framework   DIAGRAM 4-1

The Assumptions Statement is the "what if " statement. It is the statement that reflects your fundamental thinking about your venture. For instance, your thinking about the time it takes to collect the cash you are owed for invoiced sales affects not only your cash flow, but also the level of cash and accounts receivable on your balance sheet, the level of investment you need to finance your receivables, and ultimately your return on investment.

The *Core Statements* are traditionally only the Income Statement and the Balance Sheet. I've added the Cash Flow Statement to the Core group because of its critical importance to entrepreneurs, even though it can be derived from the Income Statement and Balance Sheet. In addition, entrepreneurs need to be as explicit as possible about the generation of revenues even though sales are part of the Income Statement. Consequently, a Revenue Forecast Statement is also added. Overall, the need for explicitness requires us to define four Core Statements in return for greater clarity, forecasting accuracy, and the ability to make good decisions.

To summarize, the four Core Statements for financial projections are:

1   The Sales Forecast or Revenue Statement

2   The Income Statement or Profit & Loss (P&L) Statement

3   The Balance Sheet

4   The Cash Flow Statement

The *Supporting Statements* are optional lists, schedules, and budgets that feed into specific line items of the Core Statements. Examples of Supporting Statements are a schedule of capital equipment, a schedule of debt, an R&D budget, a marketing budget, a manpower budget, etc. (See Diagram 4-2)

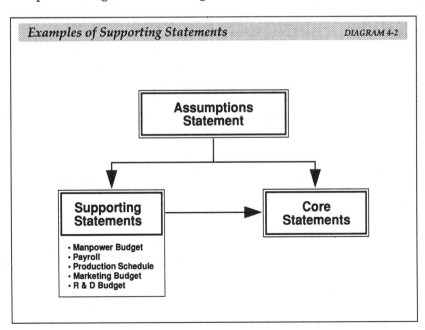

Examples of Supporting Statements   DIAGRAM 4-2

Assumptions Statement

Supporting Statements

• Manpower Budget
• Payroll
• Production Schedule
• Marketing Budget
• R & D Budget

Core Statements

The *Analytic Statements* provide valuable insight about the venture beyond that reflected in the Core Statements. Such insight may include statements of key measures (e.g., balance sheet ratios, measures of profitability or efficiency) as well as breakeven statements, percentage analysis, and valuation statements. Whereas optional Supporting Statements produce values that feed into the Core Statements, Analytic Statements contain values that are derived from the Core Statements, and possibly the Supporting Statements. (See Diagram 4-3)

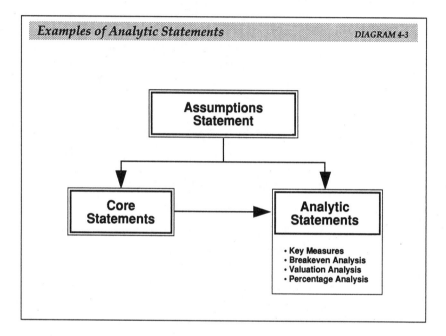

Detailed coverage of Supporting and Analytic Statements is provided in later chapters. The rest of this chapter examines the Assumptions Statement and its relationship with the Core Statements since these relationships have the greatest impact on your venture and the validity and usefulness of your projections.

The Art of Assuming

The *New World Dictionary* defines "assumption" as "the art of assuming." I believe the forgotten word in this definition is "art," since it is your artistic ability to make good assumptions that enables you to make good decisions. After all, the determinants of the accuracy and validity of your financial projections can be distilled to two factors: your ability to mathematically produce a technically sound set of linked financials, and your ability to make sound assumptions. Ronstadt's FINANCIALS handles the former; what we need to discuss now is your appreciation of the latter and your courage to make assumptions.

The Need to Make Assumptions

Every number in every statement represents an underlying assumption about your venture. Often these assumptions are unstated or partially stated in conventional accounting statements. Sometimes some of the assumptions are shown as "notes to the financial statements." All too often they are left unstated. Such full or partial omissions make it impossible for readers to understand how your venture financials were derived. Poorly stated assumptions also make it difficult (sometimes impossible) for you to follow your own projections after you've been away from them for a short time. Perhaps even more harmful is when unstated or vague assumptions are left unchanged even though conditions affecting your venture have changed.

"It is tough to predict, especially about the future!"
Sam Goldwyn

Financial projections are statements about the future. Inevitably, statements about the future *always* require assumptions. As obvious as this statement may be, it is astounding how many people are reluctant to make assumptions. Perhaps the ultimate irony regarding the development of financial projections is that the group who is least comfortable making assumptions, in my experience, is the group asked most often by enterprise leaders to make them — namely, accountants.

Today many business people depend on their accountants to generate financial proformas for them. The problem with this arrangement is that accountants are used to making precise calculations with actual or historic numbers. And believe me, I fully appreciate and admire their professional expertise and precision with historical data. But "accounting for every penny" year after year has a way of making professional accountants back away from assumption making, especially when it comes to making assumptions about an uncertain future. Of course, accountants are not the only ones who shy away from making assumptions. But whether working with practicing accountants or others, it is not uncommon to hear "We can't figure that out," or "We can't find any way to get that information," or flat out "We can't do that" — statements that, loosely translated, mean "I'm afraid to make an assumption, (often because the precise data are not available) and rather than do so, I'm going to stop right here."

All this avoidance and reluctance is unnecessary if only we engrain the following rules into our thinking:

- Assumptions are natural and necessary.
- Assumptions do NOT have to be precise.

Once these rules are accepted and made part of your thinking, you will experience not only greater comfort making assumptions but you will become freer when considering new opportunities. In fact, the very act of making assumptions represents the first step in taking control of your decision-making life.

The next step about assumption making is to be explicit and organized about it. And being explicit and organized about our assumptions is more than just better housekeeping. There is a more important reason than tidiness. This reason concerns good decision making and the need to compare not only financial results but also financial assumptions. This reason is truer today than ever before because of the computer. Compared to manual calculations, the microcomputer lets us change our assumptions quickly and instantly see the results of our thinking. But you need to know the assumptions underlying each financial scenario and be able to present these assumptions to team members, investors, bankers, and others who have a stake in your venture. People who are active practitioners and students of entrepreneurship will tell you that *your assumptions are more important than the numbers themselves*.

Components of the Assumptions Statement

The Assumptions Statement is divided into several parts in our framework ... assumptions that relate specifically to deriving the Core Financial Statements, versus any assumptions needed to produce the Supporting and Analytic Statements. The assumptions for the Supporting and Analytic Statements are optional in the sense that you don't necessarily need to fill them out to produce the Core Statements. We will wait to discuss them in a later chapter. Right now, let's focus on the assumptions needed to produce the Core Statements.

There are four sets of assumptions, each directly related to one or more of the Core Statements. These include:

- Sales Revenue Assumptions
- Income Statement Assumptions
- Balance Sheet Assumptions
- Cash Flow Assumptions

For instance, the following set of assumptions is for a new software venture where the projections are organized on a monthly basis. These assumptions are needed to generate a fairly extensive set of financial projections. Study these assumptions carefully, along with their derivations (described below) since we will use them and their assumed values in the next chapter to understand how the Core Statements are developed and linked together. (See Diagram 4-4)

Let me make a couple of observations about the role of assumptions generally (and how they operate in Ronstadt's FINANCIALS).

1   An assumption exists for the value of every item in every statement. However, many numbers within the Core Statements are derived internally (mainly by adding two or more line items "within" the same statement). Consequently, the actual number of items driven *directly* by assumptions is considerably less than all the line items in all four Core Statements.

2   Many values for the software venture are assumed to be constants. For instance, the 10% Growth Rate and 5% Returns under Sales Assumptions are noted only once under the first month (rather than tediously copying the same number for every month), because they are assumed to be the same (a constant). Starting Price Increases operate differently because we are assuming the need "to vary" the price. A 10% increase in price is shown in Month #2. In Ronstadt's FINANCIALS treating an assumption's value as something that varies is called "turning on the time series." All the other assumptions for the software venture are assumed to be constants across the monthly time periods except Fixed Assests Purchased where an additional $25,000 are bought in Month #2, then zero thereafter.

Of course, we can change the value of any of the initial assumptions. Every time we do so, the values of all other line items are recalculated in all four Core Statements.

We can also alter the assumptions in several ways. For instance, we can assume that the Unit Growth Rate will increase from 10% to 20% in later months instead of assuming the constant 10% show above, or that Cost Per Unit Sold will decrease form $10 to $9 in Month #6, due to volume economies. Also the list of assumptions can be expanded or contracted depending on the level of detail you need to show in your financial projections, For instance, Sales Assumptions can include a breakdown by product line or individual

Assumption Statement — Software Venture

REVENUE FORECAST ASSUMPTIONS:	Month 1 Software	Month 2 Software	Month 3 Software
Unit Sales:			
Unit sold month 1	1,000		
Unit growth rate	10%		
Starting price	$100		
Price increases	0%	10%	0%
Returns	5%		
INCOME STATEMENT ASSUMPTIONS:			
Cost per unit sold	$10.00		
Monthly Operating Expenses:			
Payroll	$20,000		
Payroll growth rate	5%		
Sales commissions	10%		
Shipping costs per unit	$2		
Office expenses	$25,000		
Income rate	12%		
Income tax rate (Fed & State)	41%		
BALANCE SHEET ASSUMPTIONS:			
(Optional: Enter data now for "Base Period" on the Balance Sheet Statement if you have an Opening Balance Sheet.)			
Fixed Assets Purchased:	$10,000	$25,000	$0
CASH FLOW STATEMENT ASSUMPTIONS:			
Monthly Sales Collected:			
% Collected at time of sale	10%		
% Collected 0-30 days	40%		
% Collected 31-60 days	40%		
% Collected 61-90 days	5%		
% Collected 90+ days	5%		
Monthly Expenses, Invty, F/A Paid:			
% Paid 0-30 days	30%		
% Paid 31-60 days	30%		
% Paid 61-90 days	20%		
% Paid 90+ days	20%		
Minimum Bank Deposits Required	$3,000		
Debt Payments	$1,000		
Additional Funding:			
Additional equity investments	$0	$0	
Additional debt borrowed	$0	$0	

Diagram 4-4

Assumption Statement — Retail Company

	1/31/88 Retail Comp	2/29/88 Retail Comp	3/31/88 Retail Comp
REVENUE FORECAST ASSUMPTIONS:			
Annual Sales, Store A	$700,000		
Annual Sales, Store B	$600,000		
Annual Sales, Store C	$800,000		
Percent Of Sales Allocated Per Month	5.0%	6.0%	7.0%
Sum Of "Percent Of Sales Allocated" Row	100.0%		
Growth Rate Next Year:			
Growth rate store A	10%		
Growth rate store B	5%		
Growth rate store C	5%		
INCOME STATEMENT ASSUMPTIONS:			
Cost Of Goods: (as a percent of sales)			
Store A	49.00%		
Store B	44.00%		
Store C	46.00%		
Store A: Monthly Operating Expenses			
Store A manager's salary	$1,700		
Salespeople salaries:			
Base salaries	$1,000		
Commission rate	10.00%		
Advertising and promotion, store A	3.00%		
Rent, store A	$2,000		
Supplies, store A	2.00%		
Telephone, utilities, insurance, A	$400		
Store B: Monthly Operating Expenses			
Store B manager's salary	$1,800		
Salespeople salaries:			
Base salary	$750		
Sales commission rate	11.00%		
Advertising and promotion, store B	3.00%		
Rent, store B	$2,500		
Supplies, store B	3.00%		
Telephone, utilities, insurance, B	$300		
Store C: Monthly Operating Expense			
Store C manager's salary	$1,950		
Salespeoples salaries:			

Diagram 4-5A

Assumption Statement
Retail Company

	1/31/88 Retail Comp	2/29/88 Retail Comp	3/31/88 Retail Comp
Depreciation Schedule:			
Store Fixed Assets In Years...	7		
Office Fixed Assets In Years...	5		
CASH FLOW ASSUMPTIONS:			
Base Period Accounts Receivable Received...	100%	0%	0%
Monthly Sales Collected:			
% Collected 0 - 30 days...	100%		
% Collected 31 - 60 days...	0%		
% Collected 61 - 90 days...	0%		
% Collected 90+ days...	0%		
Total Monthly Sales Collected...	100%		
Base Period Accounts Payable Paid...	100%	0%	0%
Monthly Expenses Paid:			
% Paid 0 - 30 days...	50%		
% Paid 31 - 60 days...	50%		
% Paid 61 - 90 days...	0%		
% Paid 90+ days...	0%		
Total Monthly Expenses Paid...	100%		
Vendor Deposits Required...	$0	$4,000	$1,000
Line of Credit:			
Annual line of credit interest rate...	12.00%		
Maximum line of credit...	$75,000		
Notes Payable:			
Annual note interest rate...	12.00%		
Term of note in months...	60		
Minimum Cash Balance...	$10,000		
Additional Funding:			
New equity...	$0	$45,000	$0
New debt (notes payable)...	$0	$0	$50,000

Diagram 4-5C

Assumption Statement
Retail Company

	1/31/88 Retail Comp	2/29/88 Retail Comp	3/31/88 Retail Comp
Salary base...	$500		
Commission percentage rate...	12.00%		
Advertising and promotion, store C...	4.00%		
Rent store C...	$3,000		
Supplies store C...	3.00%		
Telephone, utilities, insurance, C...	$450		
Store Payroll Tax And Benefit Rate...	10.00%		
Monthly Corporate Operating Expenses:			
Monthly administrative salaries:			
Salaries, officers...	$5,000		
Salaries, administrative...	$4,000		
Office payroll tax and benefit rate...	12.00%		
Monthly office expenses:			
Franchise fee...	0%		
Freight and postage...	$300		
Office supplies...	$1,000		
Professional fees...	$750		
Rent and occupancy...	$1,000		
Telephone...	$500		
Travel...	$1,000		
BALANCE SHEET ASSUMPTIONS:			
Inventory Purchases:			
Enter the minimum purchasing lead-time, in months, needed to receive inventory...	3		
If you entered a lead-time for purchases review your inventory on hand. You may need to increase or reduce purchases. Your adjustments may be entered below:			
Inventory adjustments store A...	$0	$0	$0
Inventory adjustments store B...	$0	$0	$0
Inventory adjustments store C...	$0	$0	$0
Fixed Assets Purchased:			
Fixed assets store A...	$0	$0	$0
Fixed assets store B...	$0	$5,000	$0
Fixed assets store C...	$5,000	$0	$0
Fixed assets corporate...	$0	$1,000	$0

Diagram 4-5B

products (Product #1, Product #2, etc.). The Income Assumptions can include additional lines that break down cost per unit sold (e.g., material cost per unit sold, labor cost per unit sold, direct overhead per unit sold). Additional operating expenses (R&D, marketing, etc.) can also be included.

Another set of assumptions is shown for a retail venture that is more extensive than the software venture and is disaggregated to track sales and selected expenses for three stores. The assumptions were set up on a monthly basis for 12 periods, although only 3 months are shown here. (See Diagram 4-5)

|||||||||||||| NOTE   *It is a simple editing procedure in Ronstadt's FINANCIALS to change these descriptions from three stores to one store with three product lines if you wish.*

Some Observations about the Retail Assumptions:

1   Monthly % sales spread represents a seasonality factor. Although not shown, it peaks during the Christmas season. (The "Sum of Percent of Sales Allocated Row" is simply a check to insure that the sum of the sales spread equals 100%.)

2   Income Statement Assumptions are all assumed to be constants.

3   Several Cash Flow Assumptions are assumed to vary including New Equity and New Debt.

The Derivation of the Assumption Statement's Components

An infinite number of Assumption Statements are possible. The specific assumptions you select and the values that are entered as assumptions must come from your knowledge of your venture and industry norms that (may) place upper and lower limits over possible assumed values. Your ability to make good assumptions will depend on how well you've done your homework about your venture and the environment in which you are launching it. As Harold Geneen, the former Chairman of ITT expressed it, "To meet your goals consistently, you have to know the business. And to know the business, you have to know the numbers — cold."

Knowing the numbers begins with knowing your assumptions, both as they are expressed in numbers and in terms of having a rationale for the numbers you choose.

Thinking about Your Assumptions: What to Assume About Time?

The Assumptions Statement forces us to be explicit and organized about many assumptions, but it does not tell us how far to project into the future nor what units of time we should use.

How far into the future do you need to project? There is no set number for all ventures. Generally, I advise estimating the time needed to get through both the prestartup and the startup period (i.e. the point when the venture has stabilized to the point where it has realized at least one full year of positive operating cash flow) and then develop your projections to cover this period of time. For some ventures, the startup period may encompass a year or two. For others, it may span many years.

When the latter occurs, it generally pays to present less detail as you attempt to project farther into the future. Accurate (which usually means detailed) projections get harder the farther out we go. The hook is that entrepreneurs are often forced to project beyond their comfort horizon. For instance, bankers may insist that you project five years into the future when applying for a five-year loan to cover the life of the liability. Venture capitalists and informal investors will want to see how your venture will fare financially up to the point of harvesting or "liquidity," a point which may extend five to seven years into the future when a Sell-Out or Initial Public Offering is possible.

Fortunately, savvy investors and bankers also realize you don't possess a crystal ball . . . at least beyond one or two years. They do expect, and rightfully so, that you will do an excellent job of projecting financially what is likely to occur for the first 12 months and a good job for months 13 through 24. My advice is monthly projections for the first year and monthly or quarterly projections for the second year. After that it pays to go to annual aggregations using industry growth rates for new ventures under poor, average, and above average conditions.

Thinking About Your Assumptions: How Sensitive Are They?

Some assumptions are more important (have a greater potential impact on your venture) than others. But you may not know initially which assumptions are more important. Consequently, you should determine the sensitivity of your projections to their underlying assumptions.

Which are the more critical assumptions? We find the answer by making an assumption and then identifying the range over which the assumption value can shift without impacting significantly on the implications of the resulting financial projections. In essence, this sensitivity range reflects our inability to be precise about the future. What we want to do is identify a safe range, one where the real value for each assumption can fall without moving us outside the threshold capitalization for our venture.

For example, let's assume that in developing your balance sheet assumptions, you make the assumption that you need 60 days inventory on hand at all times. You use the resulting dollar amount of the

60 day inventory to determine in part how much money you need to start the venture. Realizing that you are not that sure of the 60 day figure, you try to find out how high the number of days of inventory can go before you need significantly more dollars than expected to start the venture. Likewise, you want to know how far you can safely reduce inventory and what impact the dollars savings have on the total amount you need to start the venture. More importantly, you should force yourself to think: Is there some way I can reduce inventory by altering the way I'm planning this venture?

What you are doing in this questioning process is trying to identify the range over which your 60 day inventory assumption can shift, without changing the implications of the projections. That is, where you require either more or less capital to start the venture than originally planned. Similarly, you need to discover the sensitivity of assumptions about discounts, returns, cost of goods, and other variables and then identify which are the most critical. In the diagram below, inventory levels above 75 days require additional capital which takes us above our band of threshold capitalization, while 45 days of inventory takes us below so that we need to raise substantially less capital. (See Diagram 4-6)

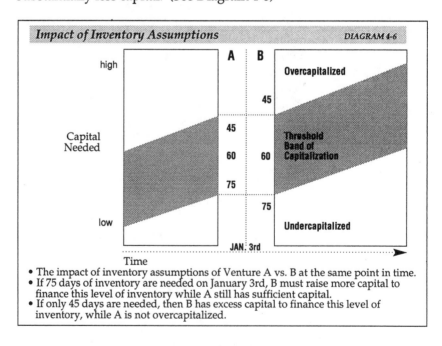

Impact of Inventory Assumptions   DIAGRAM 4-6

- The impact of inventory assumptions of Venture A vs. B at the same point in time.
- If 75 days of inventory are needed on January 3rd, B must raise more capital to finance this level of inventory while A still has sufficient capital.
- If only 45 days are needed, then B has excess capital to finance this level of inventory, while A is not overcapitalized.

As we have just seen, the identification of an assumption range (or band) for critical assumptions enables you to use the Cash Flow Statement to determine how much money you really need to start your venture as you cross over the endpoint of each assumption range.

When the "assumed" value falls outside this range, two significant impacts occur:

1 Cash flow is changed to the point you need more financing or you have excess (and expensive) financing.

2 The results shown in our Analytic Statements change to the point that accepted measures (ratios, breakevens, margins, etc.) no longer conform to industry standards or levels acceptable to investors and bankers.

Thinking About Your Assumptions: How Precise Do They Have to Be?

In preparing financial projections, you must decide what is a reasonable and meaningful level of precision for not only your results, but also for the values of your assumptions. Your understanding about how precise to be will increase as you learn about the sensitivity and importance of certain variables. Initially, the mistake most people make when generating their first projections is trying to be too precise. You don't need to round dollars to the nearest penny. Generally speaking, ballpark figures are all that's needed.

Here are some simple rules about precision:

1 Don't worry about being very precise when you take your first cut at your projections during the venture feasibility phase. It's faster to consider gross or whole values and you may discover that, even under the most liberal conditions regarding precision, you aren't interested in pursuing the selected scenario.

2 Many currency variables (except for Price) can be rounded off in hundreds or thousands for most smaller ventures.

3 Larger ventures can round currency items in ten thousands in many cases without affecting the outcome of their projections.

4 It may make sense for you to project with less detailed the further into the future you project.

Summary: Dare to Assume

The Basic Statements are composed of Core Statements, Supporting Statements, and Analytic Statements. All of these are controlled by the assumptions you make. In our framework, an overarching Assumptions Statement has been created so you can be explicit about the underlying "thinking" that has gone into your venture projections.

Because assumptions are the basis of every financial scenario, you need to spend a disproportionate amount of time *thinking* about them. Remember, your assumptions are the first and most critical links to all the other statements.

In addition to the assumptions stated in the Assumptions Statement, each set of financial projections includes several other implicit assumptions. These include the amount of time you decide to project into the future, the relevant time period (weekly, monthly, quarterly, or annually) you select for your projections, and the level of precision you decide to show in your projections.

Most importantly, don't become paralyzed by "fear of assumption making." Only by making assumptions can you generate creative venture scenarios. Think hard about your venture's assumptions. Think creatively as you puzzle through what is or should be unique about your venture vis-a-vis other ventures. Most of all, dare to assume.

Understanding Your Financial Projections

5

5

How Statements and Projections Evolve

Today's entrepreneurs need to understand how accounting statements and financial projections are created and evolve. Practically speaking, they need this knowledge to plan and execute the startup of their ventures. They also need it for their own peace of mind. The experience of one entrepreneur speaks for many:

"Numbers may be the language of commerce, but it's a dialect few of us speak when we first go into business. That can make for some very anxious moments. I recall being at the mercy of my bookkeeper for seven long years. She was oracular, and I would wait nervously for her to deliver each month's profit-and-loss statement. It took about 15 years before I actually understood the double-entry method of accounting. As much as I pretended to read, comprehend, and comment on P&Ls and balance sheets, I was operating under a thick film of ignorance that I was too embarrassed to admit. It was only later — after I got over both my ignorance and my embarrassment — that I fully appreciated the role numbers should play in the management of a successful business." [1]

Most entrepreneurs need to control their environments as much as possible given the high uncertainty that confronts them. Fortunately, reduction of uncertainty in the area of financial projections is attainable and you shouldn't have to wait years to experience it. For venturing to be truly a calculated risk, you should be calculating likely cash flows, not guessing about them. As Dr. Who, once said, "Never guess … unless you have to. There is enough uncertainty in the universe." 2

In this spirit, our immediate goal is to help you to reduce uncertainty and gain better control over your financial decisions. The first step is to make certain you understand the *general interrelationships* between the Core Financial Statements, including the Assumptions Statement. The second step is to define the basic decisionmaking blocks of financial projections, the Core Statements (i.e., the Sales Revenue Forecast Statement, the Income Statement, the Balance Sheet Statement, and the Cash Flow Statement). You need to understand their composition, use, and importance. The third step is to show you how *the specific components* of the Core Statements are linked together so you can begin to appreciate the interrelationships that the numbers represent. Here you don't need to become an expert at building complex financial models. My intent is not to make you into financial analysts. But you do need to understand how these relationships are formed and how a change in assumptions affects all the values in each venture scenario. Such knowledge will enable you to make better venture decisions.

The fact that all the numbers are related to one another is why accounting and finance aficionados refer to linked financial projections as "integrated" financial statements. But whether "integrated," "linked," or "derived," what we specifically want to know is:

- how the financial statements are related to one another as a group;
- how the individual components of each financial statement are linked together within the same statement;
- how the individual components of each financial statement are linked to components with the same or similar names on different statements; e.g., how "cash" on the Balance Sheet is linked to "cash" on the Cash Flow Statement; and,
- how the individual components of each financial statement are linked to different components in other financial statements.

In the latter two cases, we are especially interested in the number of items involved in each linkage and the direction of the association. For example, Net Income from the Income Statement and Retained Earnings from the Balance Sheet are linked together. However, we also need to know that Retained Earnings is derived from Net Income, not vice versa. We also need to know what other variables, if any, are involved (or could be involved) in the calculation; e.g., if Dividends were declared, they would have to be subtracted from Net Income and subtracted from Ending Cash on the Cash Flow Statement. (See Diagram 5-1)

Once you understand how these specific linkages work, you will be able to better understand not only what it takes to balance your balance sheet, but also how to obtain answers about the key questions of Entrepreneurial Finance.

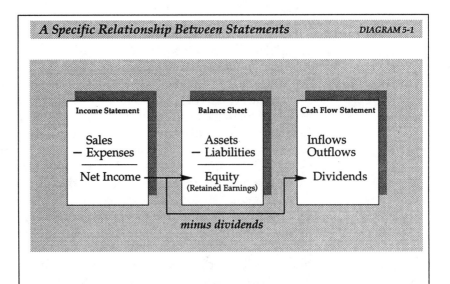

A Specific Relationship Between Statements   *DIAGRAM 5-1*

Income Statement	Balance Sheet	Cash Flow Statement
Sales − Expenses ――――― Net Income →	Assets − Liabilities ――――― Equity (Retained Earnings)	Inflows Outflows → Dividends

minus dividends

This illustration is an example of a specific relationship between net income, retained earnings and dividends.

The General Relationship Between the Core Statements

In the previous chapter, we saw the fundamental association between our assumptions and the Core Statements. Now let's examine how the Core Statements are linked together as a group. A diagram helps us to visualize these general linkages. Graphically, the relationships between the statements are shown in Diagram 5-2 as they work in Ronstadt's FINANCIALS.

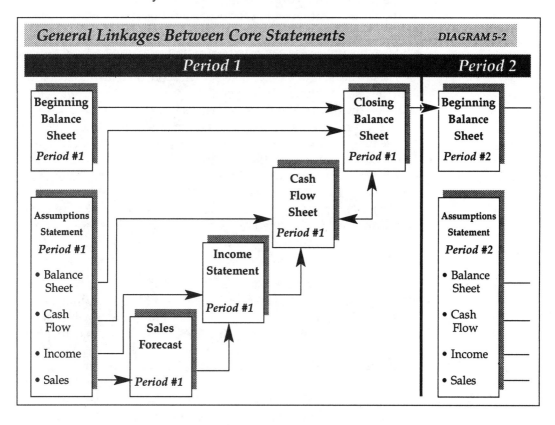

After providing information for an Assumptions Statement (including optional data for a Beginning Balance Sheet for Period #1), the diagram traces how this information flows to produce the values in the Sales Forecast, the Income Statement, the Balance Sheet, and the Cash Flow Statement. Here's how it works:

- Selected values that are produced in the Sales Forecast (e.g. Net Sales), based on data taken from the Assumptions Statement, flow directly into the Income Statement for Period #1.

- Beginning Balance Sheet values for Period #1 (if you have listed them under the "Base Period" in the Balance Sheet Statement) are combined with information for the first period from the Assumptions Statement, the Income Statement, and the Cash Flow Statement to create the values shown in the Closing Balance Sheet for Period #1.

IIIIIIIIIIIIII **NOTE**   *The Closing Balance Sheet for Period #1 becomes the Beginning Balance Sheet for Period #2 and the process continues for the total number of time periods being projected. In Ronstadt's FINANCIALS, the Base Period Balance Sheet and the Balance Sheets for the ending date of each time period are all shown as part of the Balance Sheet Statement.*

- Certain information is also flowing from the Closing Balance Sheet into the Cash Flow Statement. This information is supplemented with data drawn from the Assumptions Statement and the Income Statement to produce the values shown in the Cash Flow Statement.
- Then the process is reenacted for Period #2, Period #3, etc.

These *general relationships* between the Core Statements exist for all financial projections. However, there are many specific ways to configure the Core Statements, perhaps as many as there are different ventures. Some obvious differences exist across industries. It's one reason why Ronstadt's FINANCIALS has a library of financial statements that represent different industries. However, differences in Core Statements can also exist within the same industry. Sometimes these differences are minor and at other times they are quite significant in the number of individual items and the way individual items are derived and linked together. Consequently, there are unlimited specific kinds of financial statements and multiple ways to derive the specific linkages across statements.

What follows represents but one way. Yet, because many of the variations can be minor, it serves as a benchmark for building and linking together the components of financial projections. Since actual numbers help us to trace the linkages, let's assume you are planning to expand a small retail venture you recently started. You are using Ronstadt's FINANCIALS and you've just finished completing the Assumption Statement shown on the following pages. You've also filled out the "Base Period" or Opening Balance Sheet column on the Balance Sheet Statement. The program then computes your monthly Revenue Statement, Income Statement, Balance Sheet, and Cash Flow for the next twelve months. Each of these statements will be presented and discussed in this chapter.

Assumption Statement
Retail Company

	1/31/88 Retail	2/29/88 Retail	3/31/88 Retail	4/30/88 Retail	5/31/88 Retail	6/30/88 Retail	7/31/88 Retail	8/31/88 Retail	9/30/88 Retail	10/31/88 Retail	11/30/88 Retail	12/31/88 Retail
REVENUE FORECAST ASSUMPTIONS:												
Annual Sales, Store A	$300,000											
Percent Of Sales Allocated / Month...	4.0%	5.5%	3.5%	5.0%	9.0%	7.0%	5.0%	2.0%	4.0%	9.0%	20.0%	26.0%
Should Sum To 100%.................	100.0%											
Growth Rate Next Year:												
Growth rate store A..............	10%											
INCOME STATEMENT ASSUMPTIONS:												
Cost Of Goods as a percent of sales												
Store A	45.00%											
Store A: Monthly Operating Expenses												
Store A manager's salary	$2,500											
Salespeople salaries:												
Base salaries.................	$750											
Commission rate...............	5.00%											
Advertising and promotion, store..	3.00%											
Rent, store A..................	$1,500											
Supplies, store A.............	3.00%											
Telephone, utilities, insurance ..	$1,000											
Store Payroll Tax And Benefit Rate...	18.00%											
BALANCE SHEET ASSUMPTIONS:												
Inventory Purchases:												
Enter min. purchasing lead-time, in months to receive inventory....	2											
Please review your inventory. You may want to increase or decrease your inventory.												
Enter your adjustments below:												
Inventory adjustments store A.....	$6,300	$7,000	$0	$0	$0	$0	$0	$0	$0	$0	$0	$0
Fixed Assets Purchased:												
Fixed assets store A..........	$25,000	$0	$0	$0	$0	$0	$0	$0	$0	$0	$0	$0
Depreciation Schedule:												
Store Fixed Assets In Years...	7											
CASH FLOW ASSUMPTIONS:												
Base Period Accts Rec. Received.....	100%	0%	0%	0%	0%	0%	0%	0%	0%	0%	0%	0%

Diagram 5-3A

Assumption Statement
Retail Company

	1/31/88 Retail	2/29/88 Retail	3/31/88 Retail	4/30/88 Retail	5/31/88 Retail	6/30/88 Retail	7/31/88 Retail	8/31/88 Retail	9/30/88 Retail	10/31/88 Retail	11/30/88 Retail	12/31/88 Retail
Monthly Sales Collected:												
% Collected 0 - 30 days..........	80%											
% Collected 31 - 60 days.........	10%											
% Collected 61 - 90 days.........	5%											
% Collected 90+ days.............	5%											
Total Monthly Sales Collected......	100%	50%	10%	0%	0%	0%	0%	0%	0%	0%	0%	0%
Base Period Accounts Payable Paid....	40%											
Monthly Expenses Paid:												
% Paid 0 - 30 days...............	70%											
% Paid 31 - 60 days..............	30%											
% Paid 61 - 90 days..............	0%											
% Paid 90+ days.................	0%											
Total Monthly Expenses Paid..........	100%											
Vendor Deposits Required..........	$1,250	$0	$0	$0	$0	$0	$0	$0	$0	$0	$0	$0
Line of Credit:												
Annual line of interest rate......	12.00%											
Maximum line of credit..........	$50,000											
Notes Payable:												
Annual note interest rate.........	11.50%											
Term of note in months...........	60											
Minimum Cash Balance..............	$5,000											
Additional Funding:												
New equity.............	$15,000	$0	$0	$0		$0			$0	$0	$0	
New debt (notes payable)....	$20,000	$0	$0	$0		$0			$0	$0	$0	
PROJECTED BREAKEVEN ASSUMPTIONS:												
Variable Portion Of Cost Of Goods....	50.0%											
Variable Portion Of Store Salaries....	20.0%											
Variable Portion Of Advtg & Promo....	30.0%											

Diagram 5-3B

The assumptions made in Diagram 5-3 assume annual sales of $300,000 for Store A (eventually, you hope to start two or three more stores). The spread of sales shows a strong seasonality factor with 20% and 26% of total sales realized respectively in November and December.

|||||||||||||| NOTE   *The "Sales" formula multiplies $300,000 by each month's seasonality factor which creates projected monthly sales so that the $300,000 shown in January is not simply replicated across all twelve months for total sales of $3,600,000.*

A 10% annual growth rate is used to calculate 1989 sales which are used to figure certain 1988 items (e.g., Purchases) that need "to look into" January and February of 1989 to calculate and derive November and December values. Cost of Sales is projected at 45% of total sales based on prior experience. Operating expenses include the addition of a store manager (so we can subsequently start Store B). It also assumes an increase in advertising to 3% (from 0%). Assets are depreciated over seven years, and payroll taxes and benefits have been increased to 18% due to a new employee benefits package. Inventory requirements on hand are two months, on average.

|||||||||||||| NOTE   *The formula related to the two month lead time will show inventory purchases in Month #1, based on cost of sales in Month # 3; consequently, we need to enter our assumed inventory purchases for January and February ($6,300 and $7,000, respectively). Our cash flow assumptions show that 100% of our prior Accounts Receivables will be collected in January. These were a few known customers who were allowed to charge their purchases. However, we've decided to liberalize our policy to allow more store accounts. We believe Collections will be slower (represented by the 80%, 10%, 5%, 5% spread of Receivables over 90+ days), but will be more than offset by greater sales compared to last year.*

Prior year's payables will be paid over a three-month period with 40% paid in January, 50% in February, and 10% in March. Accounts Payables incurred in 1988 will be paid faster (70% within 30 days and 30% within 60 days) to improve credit ratings with suppliers so that good terms can be obtained when Store B is started.

An additional $25,000 in fixed assets will be purchased in January to make Store A a better place to shop. Some vendor deposits ($1,250) have been made for various deposits.

Remaining long-term debt ($20,000) is payable over five years or 60 months at 11.50%. We also have a $50,000 line of credit at 12% with our bank where we must also maintain a minimum cash balance of $5,000.

Additional Funding is set at zero for both New Equity and New Debt, so we can determine the cash needed to fund your venture (to be shown in the Cash Flow Statement). This figure will tell us if we need Additional Funding, and how much is needed. The monthly

Ending Cash Balance will indicate when these funds will be needed. We can then experiment with injecting different amounts of equity and/or debt into the venture to see what kinds of financial projections are associated with different debt/equity combinations.

In order to calculate the amount of sales the Store needs to "breakeven" for different assumptions and financial projections, we need to make rough estimates to what extent monthly costs are totally variable (100% means these costs "vary" directly with each incremental sale ... i.e., the cost is not incurred until the sale is made) versus totally fixed (0% means these costs must be paid even if nothing is sold). For example, Corporate Salaries (0%) must be paid each month even if there were no sales. As such, corporate salaries are totally fixed costs. However, Advertising and Promotion is 30% variable because the promotions portion (30%) is paid *only* when someone buys something. Advertising is 70% of the budget and it is fixed because we must pay our advertising bill even if we sell nothing.

We'll discuss "breakeven analysis" in greater detail later. For now, let's see how these assumptions are used with other variables to produce each Core Statement.

Core Statement #1: The Revenue Statement (or Sales Forecast)

The better business plans I have read over the last decade did a good job, by and large, of forecasting their costs. Usually, it is possible, though sometimes tedious, to identify cost items. For instance, you can generally obtain ballpark estimates of R&D, marketing, production, and administrative expenses, if you do your industry homework. If these "better plans" had a flaw it was their estimates of sales revenues or the "top line."

Prior to startup, "the top line" is the most important line for nearly all entrepreneurial enterprises. After startup, other lines may assume greater importance. For instance, a manufacturing enterprise that is materials intensive may need to monitor inventory and purchasing of certain materials much closer than sales (once these are known for some relevant period of time). The reason is that slight variations in materials costs can have a devastatingly negative or incredibly positive impact on profits compared to slight changes in sales. 3

But before venture launch, the top line is usually the hardest line to forecast accurately. That's why we have chosen to separate it from the income statement and give it the status of a separate statement.

Conventional knowledge, as embodied by venture capitalists at least, holds that entrepreneurs tend to overestimate the top line on a regular and consistent basis. I should emphasize that estimates of the "top line" aren't always wildly optimistic. Errors occur in both directions, as the following quotes testify.

"In 1982, Rosen and partner L.J. Sevin ... invested in a company then called Gateway Technology Inc. Gateway's plan said the company would make a portable computer compatible with IBM's personal computer and would sell 20,000 machines for $35 million in its first year — 'Which we didn't believe for a moment,' says Rosen. The sales projection for the second year was even more outrageous: $198 million. 'Can you imagine seeing a business plan like this for a company going head-on against IBM, and projecting $198 million?' he asks. He and Sevin told the fledgling company (later named Compaq) to scale down their projections." [4]

Compaq subsequently became the largest first-year growth company in history with sales over $100 million in its first twelve months of operations. "Founded in Houston in 1982, Compaq went from startup to the Fortune 500 in three years, faster than any other new company. It is expected to post more than $1 billion in sales in 1987." [5]

Of course, errors just as extreme can be documented in the other direction. However, you should know that investors, especially the professional ones, have a clear bias to be "wildly conservative" about the top line since lower projections also lower venture valuations which gives them more equity for a given level of investment.

In the midst of all this bias among entrepreneurs and investors, ignorance still rules supreme. Our knowledge of entrepreneurship has mushroomed over the last decade. However, I am not aware of any factual knowledge about the actual direction or magnitude of error for estimating sales in new ventures. Nor are there any systematic studies that have examined what constitutes an "acceptable error" for different kinds of startups in different industries. Nevertheless, you will need to estimate what represents an acceptable error since nearly all of us "err" to some extent.

What is an "acceptable error?" In the absence of specific evidence I can only give you some broad guidelines about making assumptions; but the general rule is that an acceptable error is one that does not impact materially the venture's viability. A more specific rule is that an acceptable error is equivalent to the range of sales your venture's cash flow can tolerate without requiring additional debt or equity investment. Both unexpected sales growth or sales decline can cause an increase in cash needs that push you above the upper limit of your venture's threshold capitalization. For instance, you need to know the maximum sales increase for which you have sufficient cash to cover related increases in costs and cash outflows that may suddenly begin increasing at a rate faster than cash inflows.

Conversely, you need to know the maximum sales declines for which you have sufficient cash to cover decreases in cash inflows that may be occurring faster than the decline in costs and cash outflows.

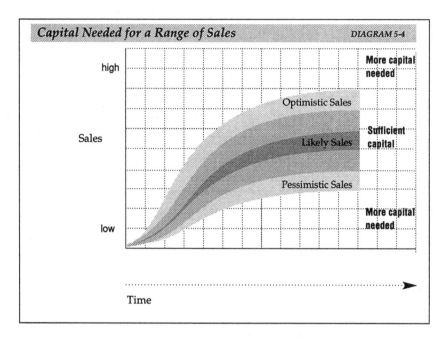

The shaded portion of Diagram 5-4 represents a range of sales. Our ultimate task (in terms of Entrepreneurial Finance) is to discover what is the appropriate amount of capital that will finance not just Likely Sales, but the entire range of sales possibilities between Pessimistic and Optimistic Sales Forecasts.

The Components of the Sales Revenue Statement

The basic components of a Sales Revenue Statement can vary from one to many items. They may include no more than a single line (e.g. Net Sales) if you are doing a quick feasibility analysis as is the case for our retail venture. (See Diagram 5-5)

Of course, many additional components can be involved for a more detailed forecast of sales. The following example is slightly more complicated insofar as it breaks out "deductions." More extensive calculations of sales break down "units" and "prices" for different products and services; and/or disaggregate sales by location (store A, Store B, etc) or channel of distribution, or any number of other ways.

Revenue Forecast
Retail Company

	1/31/88 Retail	2/29/88 Retail	3/31/88 Retail	4/30/88 Retail	5/31/88 Retail	6/30/88 Retail	7/31/88 Retail	8/31/88 Retail	9/30/88 Retail	10/31/88 Retail	11/30/88 Retail	12/31/88 Retail	Year 1 Retail
Sales, Store A............	$12,000	$16,500	$10,500	$15,000	$27,000	$21,000	$15,000	$6,000	$12,000	$27,000	$60,000	$78,000	$300,000
Net Sales.................	$12,000	$16,500	$10,500	$15,000	$27,000	$21,000	$15,000	$6,000	$12,000	$27,000	$60,000	$78,000	$300,000
Monthly Inc (Dec) In Sales...	0%	38%	(36%)	43%	80%	(22%)	(29%)	(60%)	100%	125%	122%	30%	N/A

Diagram 5-5

Sales Breakdown

	Period #1	Period #2
Units	XXX	XXX
Price	XXX	XXX
Gross Sales	XXX	XXX
Deductions	XXX	XXX
Net Sales	XXX	XXX

The relationship between these items and how they are expressed is as follows:

Relationships Between Items

Units . . . . Expressed in absolute numbers
For service businesses, units are often
expressed in hours, days, numbers of clients, etc.

Times:

Price . . . . Expressed in dollars per Unit.

Equals:

Gross Sales . . . . . Derived by multiplying Price times Units.

Minus:

Deductions . . . . Expressed in dollars.

Equals:

Net Sales . . . . .Derived by subtracting deductions
from Gross Sales.

It is quite possible to expand or contract this statement and alter the terminology to make it consistent with other kinds of ventures. For instance, we could replace "Sales" with "Billings" for certain kinds of professional service ventures. Or we could break down "Deductions" to distinguish between "discounts, royalties, returns, damaged goods," etc. But the basic structure remains relatively the same.

The Derivation of the Sales Forecast's Components

In the example above:

Units

Units are taken from the Assumptions Statement in one of two ways. Over time, the number of units is the product of assumptions made about: a) the number of units sold for the first period (month, quarter, or year) multiplied by an assumed growth rate for subsequent time periods; or b) a separate assumption is made for the number of units sold for each or selected time periods; e.g., the number of units does or does not grow at some growth rate for 5 months, then in month 6, the number of units sold triples, followed by no growth for 4 months, then the number of units sold doubles, etc. Whichever the case, a specific assumption is needed about Units on the Assumptions Statement.

Price

Price is taken from the Assumptions Statement. Like Units, Price can be assumed to change over time either by using a price growth factor or simply inserting each price increase or decrease for every time period.

Deductions

Deductions are taken from the Assumptions Statement as either an absolute number based on personal or industry experience or as a percentage of Gross Sales.

From the information about Units, Price, and Deductions, Gross Sales and Net Sales are derived internally.

For our retail venture, we've decided not to make these distinctions since these projections represent our first cut to see if the venture expansion is feasible. We'll get more refined later. Right now we're simply going to look at the venture for different sales levels. Based on some preliminary work, we think $300,000 in annual sales represents a realistic "top line." In our Assumptions Statement, we assumed a seasonality spreading of these sales. Consequently, monthly sales in Diagram 5-5 are derived in the Revenue Statement simply by multiplying our Annual Sales assumption by the monthly seasonality factor.

Core Statement #2: The Income Statement

The Income Statement presents your venture's performance over a specified period of time (be it a month, quarter, or year) in terms of sales, costs, and profits or losses. A "projected" Income Statement's main purpose is to show how much profit (or loss) you expect to earn based on when you make your sales and incur your costs, as opposed to when you actually collect the cash for the sales or paid for the costs you are obligated to pay.

A great many ventures begin their lives "in the red" or showing losses at least until they reach the startup period and even then losses are not uncommon for some period of time. The exceptions include: a) the new venture that starts with a customer who has prepaid for a product or service before any expenses are incurred; or b) the existing venture that is expanding into new territory but has sufficient revenues and cash flow from ongoing activities to cover the "new venture," which is incorporated into the existing accounting system of the business. The vast majority of new ventures, however, do not realize sales during their pre-startup periods, only costs that translate into losses without any revenues to offset them.

Components of the Income Statement

The principal components are sales, costs, and profits.

Sales - Costs =
Profits

Costs are often divided into two groups: "Cost of Goods Sold" (or "Cost of Sales" for non-product ventures) represents the *direct costs* to produce or acquire (via subcontracting) the venture's products or services. These direct costs are subtracted from Net Sales to yield Gross Profit. Then other *indirect costs* (usually called "Operating Expenses" or simply "Expenses") are subtracted from Gross Profit to yield Profit Before Taxes. Income Taxes are then subtracted to yield Net Profit, unless the venture is organized as a sole proprietorship, partnership, or S-Corporation. In these instances, there are no tax impacts at the venture level. Here profits are distributed to the owner(s) and taxed at the personal level.

The Income Statement for our retail store is shown in Diagram 5-6.

Each of these items is defined as follows:

Net Sales

Net Sales has already been defined; however, I should add that both Gross Sales and Net Sales are recognized when a customer receives legal ownership or licensing rights to the product or service being sold ... not when cash is received for the product or services, though these two events sometimes coincide.

Cost of Sales

Cost of Sales includes the "direct costs" of producing a product or providing a service during the forecasting period. By direct costs, we mean the costs of materials, labor, and selected overhead costs that are "directly" associated with the goods or services being sold.

Income Statement
Retail Company

	1/31/88 Retail	2/29/88 Retail	3/31/88 Retail	4/30/88 Retail	5/31/88 Retail	6/30/88 Retail	7/31/88 Retail	8/31/88 Retail	9/30/88 Retail	10/31/88 Retail	11/30/88 Retail	12/31/88 Retail	Year Retail
Net Sales.............	$12,000	$16,500	$10,500	$15,000	$27,000	$21,000	$15,000	$6,000	$12,000	$27,000	$60,000	$78,000	$300,000
Cost of Goods........	5,400	7,425	4,725	6,750	12,150	9,450	6,750	2,700	5,400	12,150	27,000	35,100	135,000
Gross Profit	6,600	9,075	5,775	8,250	14,850	11,550	8,250	3,300	6,600	14,850	33,000	42,900	165,000
Operating Expenses:													
Salaries and wages........	4,543	4,809	4,455	4,720	5,428	5,074	4,720	4,189	4,543	5,428	7,375	8,437	63,720
Occupancy................	2,500	2,500	2,500	2,500	2,500	2,500	2,500	2,500	2,500	2,500	2,500	2,500	30,000
Advertising and promotion...	360	495	315	450	810	630	450	180	360	810	1,800	2,340	9,000
Supplies	360	495	315	450	810	630	450	180	360	810	1,800	2,340	9,000
Depreciation.............	714	714	714	714	714	714	714	714	714	714	714	714	8,571
Total operating expense.....	8,477	9,013	8,299	8,834	10,262	9,548	8,834	7,763	8,477	10,262	14,189	16,331	120,291
Operating Profit (Loss).........	(1,877)	62	(2,524)	(584)	4,588	2,002	(584)	(4,463)	(1,877)	4,588	18,811	26,569	44,709
Other Expenses / Income.........	288	476	486	621	665	597	524	496	587	775	920	733	7,168
Income Before Income Taxes	$(2,165)	$(413)	$(3,010)	$(1,205)	$3,922	$1,405	$(1,108)	$(4,959)	$(2,464)	$3,812	$17,890	$25,835	$37,540

Diagram 5-6

Gross Profit

Gross Profit is simply Net Sales minus Cost Of Sales. However, Gross Profit and its percentage equivalent, Gross Margin, should not be confused with "Gross Contribution" or "Contribution Margin." Just as Net Sales does not necessarily mean "Cash Sales," so Gross Profit is not always the equivalent of "Contribution" or "Contribution Dollars." For now, it is sufficient to know that the distinction is important and covered later when we discuss "contribution analysis."

Operating Expenses

Operating Expenses includes all other costs (payroll, marketing expenses, R&D expenses, general and administrative costs, depreciation, etc.) that are incurred with ongoing operation of the venture. Excluded are long term financing expenses that are related to establishing the venture as opposed to operating it. Also excluded are taxes on profits plus any extraordinary costs that do not tend to recur on a regular basis.

Operating Profit

Operating Profit is Gross Profit minus Operating Expenses or the profit earned from "operating the venture" as opposed to any profit earned from other sources (e.g., the interest income received from cash in savings accounts or other interest bearing instruments).

Other Expenses/Income

Other Expenses/Income represents the net of other costs and profits that are not associated with the operation of the primary activities of the venture. In our Retail Store, year-end interest expense is $7922.

Income Before Income Taxes

Income Before Income Taxes is simply Operating Profit minus Other Expenses/Income. Income Taxes include only State and Federal taxes on income. Other kinds of taxes (local real estate taxes, withholding taxes, etc.) are included in Operating Expenses.

Our retail example shows no state or federal income taxes because it is organized as an S-Corporation. Let's assume for a moment that the Store is a C-Corporation and is subject to income taxes. Then:

1   Two new lines would have to be inserted — Income Taxes and Net Income After Tax on the Income Statement.

2   One new line would have to be inserted — Income Tax Rate — on the Assumptions Statement (under Income Statement Assumptions) and a rate entered.

Finally, let me emphasize that Net Profit After Tax is *not* Net Cash Flow. Net Profit represents an "accounting profit." You may show an accounting profit for a given month and have still never collected a dime in hard cash and/or actually paid for the expenses you've incurred on your Income Statement.

The Derivation of the Income Statement's Components

In our Retail Store example several items (Gross Profit, Total Operating Expenses, Operating Profit, and Net Income Before Taxes) are calculated internally from other Income Statement items. Also, we've already seen how one item, Net Sales, has been simply copied from the Revenue Statement. The actual values are show in Diagram 5-6.

The remaining five items are all derived as follows:

||||||||||||||| NOTE   *The source of each item is shown in parentheses when it comes from a Core Statement other than the Income Statement.*

Cost of Goods
Cost of Goods is calculated by multiplying Net Sales by Cost of Goods Percentage for Store A (45%) (Assumptions Statement).

Salaries and Wages
Salaries and Wages is calculated by adding Payroll and Payroll Taxes and Benefits. First, Payroll is derived by adding the Store Manager Salaries (Assumption Statement) the result of Net Sales (Income Statement) times the 5% Commission Rate (Assumptions Statement), plus the base salary. Then, taxes and benefits are calculated by multiplying payroll by the 18% Store Payroll Tax and Benefit Rate (Assumptions Statement).

Occupancy
Occupancy is calculated by adding monthly Rent (Assumptions Statement) plus monthly Telephone Utilities, and Insurance (Assumptions Statement).

Advertising and Promotion
Advertising and Promotion is calculated by multiplying Net Sales by the 3% monthly Advertising Rate (Assumptions Statement).

Supplies and Other

Supplies and Other is calculated by multiplying Net Sales by the 3% monthly Supplies Rate (Assumptions Statement).

Depreciation

Depreciation is calculated in this instance by using a straightline depreciation function that is equivalent to taking the $60,000 of Total Property and Equipment at Cost (Balance Sheet) for Period #1 and dividing it by seven years, the Store Fixed Assets Depreciation Rate (Assumptions Statement) and then dividing this total ($8,571) by 12 months to arrive at the $714 of Monthly Depreciation shown on the Income Statement.

Interest Expense/Income

Interest Expense/Income is calculated by multiplying the Beginning Principal Balance (Cash Flow Statement) times the 11.5% Annual Interest Rate (Assumptions Statement) divided by 12 months plus previous month Line of Credit (Balance Sheet) times the 12% Line of Credit Interest Rate (Assumptions Statement) divided by 12 months.

Core Statement #3: The Balance Sheet

A balance sheet is a statement of the financial position of a venture at a specific point in time. It gives a snapshot of the venture's financial position at this time, expressed either in terms of historical costs for an accounting statement or future costs when a balance sheet is used for financial projections. Often the date of a balance sheet coincides with the *ending* date of an income statement; however, you should remember that the income statement is showing sales, expenses, and profit activity *over a specified period* while the balance sheet is showing the venture's financial position *exclusively as of the ending date*.

Balance Sheets are composed of three main elements: Assets, Liabilities, and Equities. Assets are resources that a firm uses to generate future earnings. Assets can be anything of value or anything legally due the venture. Liabilities are borrowings used to fund the operation of a venture. These debts may come from banks (loans) or creditors (accounts payable) or expenses incurred but not yet due or paid (payroll, income taxes, etc.). Equities are the claims that owner(s) have on the assets of the venture that remain after subtracting liabilities. Equity is also known as "Net Worth."

Assets - Liabilities = Equities

and also

Assets = Liabilities + Equities

The purpose of a balance sheet is to show the assets and liabilities you've actually employed to start your venture, or to show the assets and liabilities you will employ to start work on your venture. What is or isn't left over is equity. Remember, equity can be positive, negative, or zero. If assets equal liabilities, then your venture has zero equity. If liabilities exceed assets, then you have negative equity. Positive equity results only when assets are greater than liabilities. Of course, the objective for most entrepreneurs is to increase venture equity so it is positive.

Another way to think about it is:

1   The asset side of a proforma balance sheet shows "what it will take (in assets) to do what you want to do (given projected sales, costs, and cash flows); while

2   The liability side shows you … "where you will get, what it will take (in liabilities), to do what you want to do … and what you will get (total equity or net worth) for your efforts."

Actually, there are at least two balance sheets you need to consider when generating a set of linked financial projections: one is the Opening Balance Sheet and the other is a Closing Balance Sheet. The Opening Balance Sheet contains all prior transactions, and is sometimes called the Base Period or Beginning Balance Sheet. The Closing Balance Sheet, as the latter name suggests, shows the status of your assets, liabilities, and equities at the end of a specified period.

One reason you need two balance sheets on the Balance Sheet Statement is the fact that the other Core Statements encompass or cross some period of time. However, the balance sheet is different. It shows the status of an enterprise at a specific point in time, e.g., on January 1, 1990, when you first committed some significant dollar resources to your venture. It's vital to recognize at least two balance sheets because the comparison of the two statements allows us to understand how an organization changed the size and deployment of its assets and liabilities during the time period.

The opening balance sheet is unique because it represents either:

- a statement of historical fact ... e.g., I've started working on this venture and here are the assets I've allocated and the liabilities I've incurred, and the equity I've invested up to this point in time; or

- an assumption about the future set of assets, liabilities, and equity I will bring to the initiation of the venture.

If the latter, you may ask, "Then why isn't the opening balance sheet part of the balance sheet assumptions in the Assumptions Statement?" The answer is that it could be included in the Assumptions Statement. However, convention and convenience require us to show the Opening Balance Sheet (or at least some "Base Period") on the Balance Sheet Statement so it can be compared easily with other projected balance sheets.

What the initial time point of an Opening Balance Sheet should be for a new venture is a matter of judgement. To be informative one usually waits until some assets have been obtained and deployed. The key point is that every venture has an Opening Balance Sheet. Even if you aren't explicit about its existence, an implicit balance sheet exists. Theoretically, one exists from the point you first had the idea for your venture ... even if you had zero assets invested and zero liabilities incurred at that point.

Obviously, listing a balance sheet with zero assets and liabilities is not very informative; consequently, it usually pays to select a "base period" to mark the beginning point of your business for comparative purposes. The fact that the "base period" is not necessarily the first balance sheet does not matter for our purposes, since a balance sheet captures all that has transpired financially, up to that point in time.

For instance, Base Period #5 in Diagram 5-7 incorporates all prior balance sheet transactions, covering a 60-day pre-startup period for a venture. See if you can explain the transactions to yourself. Then read on.

	Day 1	Day 15	Day 30	Day 45	Day 60
Opening Balance Sheet or Base Period					**Diagram 5-7**
	Period #1	Period #2	Period #3	Period #4	Period #5
Cash	$ 0	$ 10,000	$ 20,000	$ 20,000	$ 15,000
Inventory	0	0	0	5,000	5,000
Fixed Assets	0	0	0	0	5,000
TOTAL ASSETS	$ 0	$ 10,000	$ 20,000	$ 25,000	$ 25,000
Trade Payables	0	0	0	5,000	5,000
Long-Term Debt	0	0	10,000	10,000	10,000
Equity	0	10,000	10,000	10,000	10,000
TOTAL LIABILITIES AND EQUITY	$ 0	$ 10,000	$ 20,000	$ 25,000	$ 25,000

IDEA FOR VENTURE	PRE-STARTUP PERIOD	60 DAYS LATER
	(NO SALES)	

Period #1:
The end of Day 1 marks the birth of your venture idea. Nothing has happened yet in the way of financial transactions, but an implicit Balance Sheet already exists.

Period #2:
As of Day 15, the following transactions have occurred — $10,000 has been invested in the venture as *equity* and appears as $10,000 in cash on the asset side of the Balance Sheet.

Period #3:
As of Day 30, an additional $10,000 has been borrowed as long-term debt, raising total Liabilities & Equities to $20,000. Cash is increased to $20,000 on the asset side of the Balance Sheet.

Period #4:
As of Day 45, $5,000 of Trade Payables has been are incurred to finance the buildup of $5,000 worth of Inventory

Period #5:
As of Day 60, no charges occur on the Liabilities & Equities side of the Balance Sheet. However, $5,000 is used to purchase (for cash) some Fixed Assets.

While these transactions are simple, they reveal a number of important things about the Balance Sheet. These are:

1   The size of your Balance Sheet in terms of Total Assets can increase (as it did in Period #3 and #4) simply by increasing long term or short term debt.

2   Shifts can occur in assets and liabilities that have a definite impact on the amount of Cash you end up with.

The Components of the Balance Sheet

The particular components of a balance sheet for any two ventures will vary based on the individual needs of specific ventures, as well as particular conventions of their respective industries. But regardless of what specific items are included and what they are called, the majority of all balance sheets have some common components. On the asset side of the balance sheet, there are three major groupings. (See Diagram 5-8)

1   *Current Assets.* These are used or could be used to finance operations within a twelve month period. Besides cash itself, current assets include items like inventory and accounts receivables that, one way or another, are expected to be converted into cash within the 12-month period.

2   *Fixed Assets.* These have an operating life longer than one year and are used to produce products and services for ongoing operations. Fixed assets, such as buildings, equipment, vehicles, and furniture are not for resale to customers. They are also sometimes called Tangible Assets.

3   *Other Assets.* These have an operating life longer than one year but do not meet the accountant's definition of fixed assets. The value of patents, trademarks, goodwill, special licenses, and other "intangibles" are classified as "other assets."

On the liabilities side of the balance sheet, one also finds three principal categories.

1   *Current Liabilities.* These are obligations that are expected to be paid within twelve months. These include items like Trade Payables, Accrued Expenses, Accrued Taxes, and the Current Portion due on any Long Term Debt.

2   *Long Term Liabilities.* These are obligations expected to be paid over periods of time greater than one year. These debts may include items like a 3-year note for equipment, a 5-year loan for vehicles, or a 15-year mortgage loan for a building.

3   *Equities.* These amounts represent the cash investment(s) contributed by the owners of the enterprise plus the net earnings retained from operations over the life of the venture.

IIIIIIIIIIIIII **NOTE**   *"Retained" earnings are "reinvested" earnings. They are not an additional asset and, specifically, retained or reinvested earnings are NOT additional cash that somehow has been left in the bottom right hand drawer.*

Balance Sheet
Retail Company

	Base Peri	1/31/88	2/29/88	3/31/88	4/30/88	5/31/88	6/30/88	7/31/88	8/31/88	9/30/88	10/31/88	11/30/88	12/31/88
ASSETS													
Current Assets:													
Cash and equivalents...	$24,700	$34,893	$5,000	$5,000	$5,000	$5,000	$5,000	$5,000	$5,000	$5,000	$610	$5,000	$19,197
Accounts receivable....	12,500	2,400	4,500	4,350	4,875	7,425	7,650	6,450	3,750	3,750	6,900	15,300	22,950
Inventories...........	7,250	12,875	19,200	26,625	29,325	23,925	17,175	15,825	25,275	46,875	69,825	48,765	21,833
Total current assets...	44,450	50,168	28,700	35,975	39,200	36,350	29,825	27,275	34,025	55,625	77,335	69,065	63,979
Property & Equipment,net..	33,500	57,786	57,071	56,357	55,643	54,929	54,214	53,500	52,786	52,071	51,357	50,643	49,929
Other Assets...........	2,500	3,750	3,750	3,750	3,750	3,750	3,750	3,750	3,750	3,750	3,750	3,750	3,750
Total Assets...........	$80,450	$111,704	$89,521	$96,082	$98,593	$95,029	$87,789	$84,525	$90,561	$111,446	$132,443	$123,458	$117,658
LIABILITIES AND EQUITY													
Current Liabilities:													
Accounts payable.......	$32,456	$31,247	$8,418	$4,584	$3,855	$3,261	$1,938	$2,640	$4,503	$9,066	$11,766	$3,612	$4,604
Accrued expenses.......	1,850	1,850	1,850	1,850	1,850	1,850	1,850	1,850	1,850	1,850	1,850	1,850	1,850
Current portion-LTD....	10,000	14,000	14,000	14,000	14,000	14,000	14,000	14,000	14,000	14,000	14,000	14,000	14,000
Line of credit........	0	0	1,676	15,702	20,775	14,516	7,835	5,622	15,406	34,852	50,000	31,950	0
Total current liab....	44,306	47,097	25,944	36,136	40,480	33,627	25,623	24,112	35,759	59,768	77,616	51,412	20,454
Long-Term Debt.........	20,000	35,628	35,012	34,390	33,762	33,129	32,489	31,843	31,191	30,533	29,868	29,197	28,519
Stockholders' Equity:													
Contributed Capital....	20,000	35,000	35,000	35,000	35,000	35,000	35,000	35,000	35,000	35,000	35,000	35,000	35,000
Retained earnings	(3,856)	(6,021)	(6,434)	(9,444)	(10,649)	(6,727)	(5,322)	(6,430)	(11,389)	(13,854)	(10,041)	7,849	33,684
Total equity..........	16,144	28,979	28,566	25,556	24,351	28,273	29,678	28,570	23,611	21,146	24,959	42,849	68,684
Total Liab & Equity......	$80,450	$111,704	$89,521	$96,082	$98,593	$95,029	$87,789	$84,525	$90,561	$111,446	$132,443	$123,458	$117,658
Does the Balance Sheet bal...	YES	YES	YES	YES	YES	YES	YES	YES	YES	YES	YES	YES	YES

Diagram 5-8

Each of these categories of assets and liabilities has additional subcategories. Our retail store example presents some of these subcategories, e.g. accounts receivables and inventory, which are also representative for a manufacturing or product business that needs to keep an inventory of goods, and invoices some or all of its sales and, therefore, must maintain accounts receivables.

The Derivation of the Balance Sheet's Components

As previously discussed, the Opening Balance Sheet for the Base Period (or Period #1) is a set of conditions and/or assumptions that exist at the point in time you are making your projections. This information is used to derive values in the Cash Flow Statement and the Closing Balance Sheet.

The derivation of the numbers for the Opening Balance Sheet come from either historical data or assumed data which are entered directly into each line item, just as sales, income, and cash flow assumptions are entered directly into the Assumptions Statement.

|||||||||||||| NOTE *Within Ronstadt's FINANCIALS, the only requirement is that the amount of total assets you enter must equal total liabilities and equities. There is no discretionary balancing or "plug" figure that automatically equalizes these totals for the Base Period. The formulas within Ronstadt's FINANCIALS are written so you do not necessarily have to enter an Opening Balance Sheet since the equalizing precondition is still satisfied when zero assets equals zero liabilities and equities.*

The derivation of the numbers for the Closing Balance Sheet is described below with the source statement for variables shown in parentheses if the variable comes from a statement other than the Balance Sheet.

Current Assets

Cash
   Cash is derived from the Ending Cash Balance (Cash Flow Statement) for the period in question.

Accounts Receivable
   Accounts Receivable is derived from the previous period's Accounts Receivables plus the current period's Net Sales (Income Statement) after subtracting Cash Received (Inflows) (Cash Flow Statement).

Inventory

Inventory is derived by adding Purchases (Supporting State-ment: Inventory Purchases) to the previous period's Inventory and then subtracting Cost Of Goods Sold (Income Statement).

Fixed Assets

Total Property and Equipment at Cost

Total Property and Equipment at Cost is calculated by adding the previous period's Fixed Assets at Cost (Balance Sheet) plus Fixed Assets Purchased (Assumption Statement).

Accumulated Depreciation

Accumulated Depreciation is calculated by adding the previous period's Accumulated Depreciation plus the current period's Depreciation (Income Statement).

Other Assets

Other Assets is calculated by adding the previous period's Other Assets (Balance Sheet) plus Vendor Deposits Made (Assumptions Statement).

Current Liabilities

Accounts Payable

Accounts Payable is calculated by taking all the previous pay-ables that you have not paid and adding all the new "bills" or obligations incurred in Operating Expenses (Income Statement) *plus* Purchases for Inventory (Inventory Purchasing Statement) *plus* Purchases of Fixed Assets (Assumptions Statement) *minus* the "bills" or obligations that do get paid during the month. Non-cash expenditures (e.g., depreciation), and payroll expenses do not flow through Accounts Payable.

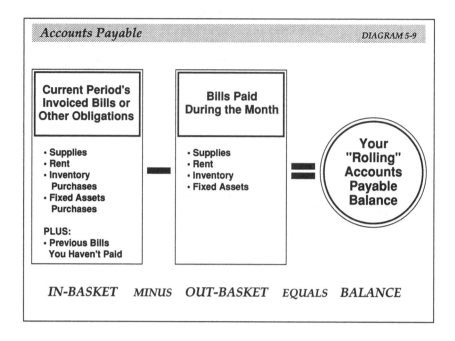

Accounts Payable   *DIAGRAM 5-9*

| Current Period's Invoiced Bills or Other Obligations | Bills Paid During the Month | Your "Rolling" Accounts Payable Balance |

- Supplies
- Rent
- Inventory Purchases
- Fixed Assets Purchases

PLUS:
- Previous Bills You Haven't Paid

- Supplies
- Rent
- Inventory
- Fixed Assets

IN-BASKET MINUS *OUT-BASKET* EQUALS *BALANCE*

Unfortunately, the formulas used to capture this process and accrued expenses can be the most complicated among those in your financial projections.

Accrued Expenses

Accrued Expenses for our Retail Store are assumed to equal the previous period's Accrued Expenses. In other situations, you may wish to include new items that are obligations you have incurred legally but have not yet received an invoice and/or are not yet obligated to pay. If so, the process is similar to Accounts Payable where old and new accrued expenses are combined and then subtracted from accrued expenses actually paid during the current period to arrive at a net accrued expenses balance.

For example, income taxes are incurred legally for each day you operate. However, you are not invoiced daily or even monthly but are expected to pay quarterly. Perhaps a better example is services you have received from a lawyer or consultant, but will not receive a bill or invoice for three or four months.

Current Portion of Long-Term Debt

Current Portion of Long-Term Debt is calculated by taking the previous period's Current Portion of Long Term Debt plus the current period's Current Portion of Long Term Debt (Cash Flow Statement) minus the Principal Payment of Long Term Debt (Cash Flow Statement) *until* Long Term Debt becomes a zero balance.

Equities

Contributed Capital

Contributed Capital is derived from the previous period's Contributed Capital (Balance Sheet) plus New Equity (Cash Flow Statement) from the current period.

Accumulated Earnings

Accumulated Earnings is derived from the previous period's Accumulated Earnings (Balance Sheet) plus Net Income Before Taxes (Income Statement) minus Dividends (Cash Flow Statement) for the current period.

Getting that Blasted Balance Sheet to Balance !!!

If you ever tried to put together a set of financial projections, you probably experienced some trying moments attempting to discover why your balance sheet didn't balance.

Don't worry. You're not alone. I've seen experienced CPAs spend hours trying to figure out why a particular set of projections didn't "tie out," i.e., produce a balanced balance sheet.

Despite what people may say, getting your Balance Sheet to balance isn't easy. It's a major reason for our program, Ronstadt's FINANCIALS. You may also wonder, since we're dealing with imprecise future projections, why you need to have a Balance Sheet that balances? The answer relates to the interdependent nature of all the statements. Because the Balance Sheet is tied to the Cash Flow and ultimately all other statements, a Balance Sheet that is out-of-balance can provide the wrong answers about how much cash your venture needs, when it needs this cash, what form the cash should take, and where you should try to raise the needed funds. In short, an incorrect balance sheet can mess up your Cash Flow Statement, any number of ratios and profitability measures, your sales break-even, and any other analysis that is derived directly or indirectly from the Balance Sheet. That means just about everything, since the linkages between the statements insure that errors ripple through your entire set of projections. In addition, a small error in your Balance Sheet can compound into a bigger error with a new round of calculations for each progressive time period. Having a Balance Sheet that's just a little bit out-of-balance is like being just a little bit pregnant. With time, the situation becomes increasingly apparent and uncomfortable.

Core Statement #4: The Cash Flow Statement

The Income Statement and the Balance Sheet have dominated the attention of stockholders, and, consequently, many managers in the past. The reasons for this domination include:

a) the importance of both statements as an indicator of the organization's past performance and current position; and

b) the fact that accountants can reduce and consolidate a great deal of information from other statements into these two statements for presentation purposes.

Both the Income Statement and the Balance Sheet also satisfy the needs of managers and stockholders of larger corporations for a relatively accurate picture of an enterprise's future health, especially when combined with a few financial ratios drawn from these statements. For instance, the amount of debt your venture has incurred relative to total equity, (the debt/equity ratio) tells us the extent the owners of the venture are *financially* committed to the enterprise versus the outside creditors and bankers. Where nearly all debt is used with very little equity, we are being told there is little financial reason for the owners to stick with the venture when it experiences difficult times. They personally may have little to lose by "walking". They also have little or no further ability to use debt to help the venture through difficult times.

Over the last decade, a third statement, the Cash Flow Statement, has garnered increasing attention among entrepreneurs, and especially owner/managers of smaller businesses. The reason is straightforward. It is actually cash that keeps ventures alive and functioning. The Cash Flow Statement tracks the actual flow of cash into and out of the venture. The Income Statement and Balance Sheet can be misleading about the true existence of cash. A false picture is especially possible for new ventures, smaller ventures, and rapidly growing ventures. At some point *within* an accounting period, a venture may not have sufficient cash to continue operating, even when the Income Statement shows a substantial projected profit and the Balance Sheet projects a positive net worth and positive cash for the end of the accounting period (some months away).

This possibility is more likely to have devastating impacts when the accounting period or the projection period covers a relatively long amount of time (e.g., a quarter or especially a year). Annual Income and Balance Sheet projections have been known to show entrepreneurs rich and famous at year-end, when their ventures actually run out of funds six months before year end. For instance, monthly Cash Flow projections show a big negative cash flow in months 6, 7, 8 followed by large positive cash flows in months 9 through 12, sufficient to produce a year end positive cumulative cash flow. Unfortunately, the venture never sees month 9.

Consequently, the Cash Flow Statement is an extremely important statement for new enterprises. It not only shows how much money you need to launch the venture but also when you will need it. These are first two questions of Entrepreneurial Finance and provide the basis for answering the other three fundamental questions.

The Cash Flow Statement tracks when you actually receive cash and when you pay it out over some specified period of time. In short, its basic purposes are to tell you if you have sufficient cash to continue present and future operations, and, if not, how much cash you will need and when you will need it to keep the venture operating at some designated level.

The Cash Flow Statement is also important because it prevents you from confusing sales with cash flow unless sales are actually cash sales. It also can tell you what your minimum cash point will be over the time period in question. From a projections perspective, the Cash Flow Statement can tell you how to manage the cash you have. It gives you the insight and time to react, to decide how to spend (or not spend) cash under a variety of circumstances.

For example, your ending cash position for any particular month can be positive or negative, depending on whether you've received more cash (including your starting cash position) than you've spent. If you cannot offset negative cash flows with additional capital (debt or equity), someone will go unpaid. You may be able to live with this condition for some period of time depending on your creditors. But eventually you will be forced to take action which hopefully will turn cash flow positive in the future. This action can include a reduction in expenditures as shown on the Income Statement; i.e., reducing wages, salaries, rent, utilities, travel, etc. Or it can include changes in Balance Sheet items that free up cash; i.e., selling fixed assets, reducing your accounts receivables faster (increasing your collections), increasing your accounts payable (extending the average time you pay vendors and other creditors), or reducing the amount of cash tied up in inventory. Should these and other possible actions prove insufficient to turn cash flow positive, you may have no other choice but to sell or discontinue the venture.

The critical point, however, is that you can use Ronstadt's FINANCIALS to test the effects of these actions BEFORE they happen. This capability allows you to manage financial decisions by evaluating numerous options quickly, using a true "what if" approach to find a viable, if not the best, option available to you.

Many ventures experience negative net cash flows from their operations early in their lives because they have to spend money to "build up the business." These negative positions should be covered by the initial capital invested in the venture and other debt and equity financings that prove necessary. Eventually, however, a venture needs to earn a positive *operating* cash flow so the business cannot only stand on its own feet but presumably begin providing a return to investors from the "operations" of the venture. For instance, the diagram on the following page illustrates the typical situation for a mail order venture at startup where operating cash flows are negative at first.

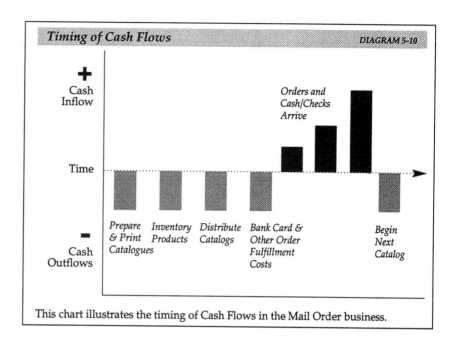

This chart illustrates the timing of Cash Flows in the Mail Order business.

Components of the Cash Flow Statement

Cash Flow Statements are arranged in many different ways. These can be categorized into at least three basic types in terms of complexity:

1 *The "Simple" Cash Flow Statement*, so-called because all items are arranged into only two categories ... cash inflows (including your starting cash position) and cash outflows.

2 *The Operating Cash Flow Statement*, so-called because cash inflows and outflows are limited initially to those cashflows that stem from the venture's ongoing "operations," as opposed to those cashflows needed to finance the venture.

3 *The Priority Cash Flow Statement*, so-called because cash inflows and particularly cash outflows are further classified into any number of priority and/or discretionary groupings.

Starting Cash +
Cash Inflows -
Cash Outflows =
Net Cash Flow

Priority Cash Flow Statements can be very useful. However their increased utility is often offset by their greater complexity. For our purposes, the Operating Cash Flow offers a better trade-off. A slight increase in complexity is worth the advantage of knowing precisely whether a positive cash flow for a particular month, quarter, or year is being produced from the venture's "operations" versus from financial inflows, or from operating inflows from *prior* periods.

Because of this advantage, I've chosen to use the Operating Cash Flow model in this book and, with slight variations, in Ronstadt's FINANCIALS. The fundamental model is shown in Diagram 5-11, fol-

lowed by the projected Cash Flow Statement for our retail venture in
Diagram 5-12.

Operating Cash Flow Statement		Diagram 5-11
	Period #1	Period #2
Cash Received:	(Inflows)	
Cash Sales	XXX	
Receivables Collected	XXX	
Operating Cash Inflows	XXX	
Cash Disbursed:	(Outflows)	
Purchases Paid	XXX	
Payroll Paid	XXX	
Other Operating Expenses Paid	XXX	
Operating Cash Outflows	XXX	
Net operating cash flow	XXX	
Non-operating inflows		
Add: Beginning Cash Balance	XXX	
New Equity Invested	XXX	
New Debt Invested	XXX	
Non-operating Outflows		
Minus: Debt Principal Payments	XXX	
Interest Payments	XXX	
Income Taxes Paid	XXX	
Fixed Assets Paid	XXX	
Dividends Paid	XXX	
Ending Cash Balance	XXX	
Cumulative Cash Flow	XXX	

Cash Flow Statement
Retail Company

	1/31/88	2/29/88	3/31/88	4/30/88	5/31/88	6/30/88	7/31/88	8/31/88	9/30/88	10/31/88	11/30/88	12/31/88
Cash Received (Inflows)												
A/R collected from 1987 Sales......	$12,500	$0	$0	$0	$0	$0	$0	$0	$0	$0	$0	$0
Monthly sales collected............	9,600	14,400	10,650	14,475	24,450	20,775	16,200	8,700	12,000	23,850	51,600	70,350
Total cash receipts................	22,100	14,400	10,650	14,475	24,450	20,775	16,200	8,700	12,000	23,850	51,600	70,350
Cash Disbursed (Outflows)												
Payroll paid.......................	4,543	4,809	4,455	4,720	5,428	5,074	4,720	4,189	4,543	5,428	7,375	8,437
A/P paid from 1987 Expenses........	12,982	16,228	3,246	0	0	0	0	0	0	0	0	0
Monthly expenses, invty, F/A paid:												
1-30 days paid.................	27,472	12,068	10,696	8,995	7,609	4,522	6,160	10,507	21,154	27,454	8,428	10,743
31-60 days paid................	0	11,774	5,172	4,584	3,855	3,261	1,938	2,640	4,503	9,066	11,766	3,612
61-90 days paid................	0	0	0	0	0	0	0	0	0	0	0	0
90+ days paid..................	0	0	0	0	0	0	0	0	0	0	0	0
Vendor deposits	1,250	0	0	0	0	0	0	0	0	0	0	0
Total cash disbursement............	46,247	44,878	23,568	18,299	16,892	12,857	12,818	17,336	30,200	41,948	27,569	22,792
Operating Cash Surplus (Deficit)......	(24,147)	(30,478)	(12,918)	(3,824)	7,558	7,918	3,382	(8,636)	(18,200)	(18,098)	24,031	47,558
Less: Interest Payments:												
Interest on debt (notes payable)....	288	476	470	464	458	452	446	439	433	427	420	414
Interest on line of credit	0	0	17	157	208	145	78	56	154	349	500	320
Less: Notes Payable Principal Payment..	372	616	622	628	634	640	646	652	658	665	671	677
Add: Beginning Of Month Cash Balance..	24,700	34,893	5,000	5,000	5,000	5,000	5,000	5,000	5,000	5,000	5,000	5,000
Cash Balance Before Funding..........	$(107)	$3,324	$(9,026)	$(72)	$11,259	$11,681	$7,212	$(4,784)	$(14,446)	$(14,538)	$23,050	$51,147
Line of Credit Principal Repayments.....	0	0	0	0	6,259	6,681	2,212	0	0	0	18,050	31,950
Additional Funding:												
New equity..........................	15,000	0	0	0	0	0	0	0	0	0	0	0
New debt (notes payable)............	20,000	0	0	0	0	0	0	0	0	0	0	0
Line of credit borrowings...........	0	1,676	14,026	5,072	0	0	0	9,784	19,446	15,148	0	0
Ending Cash Balance.................	$34,893	$5,000	$5,000	$5,000	$5,000	$5,000	$5,000	$5,000	$5,000	$610	$5,000	$19,197
Is Additional Funding Required?......	NO	NO	NO	NO	NO	NO	NO	NO	YES	YES	NO	NO

If YES, please enter your amount in
the "New equity" or "New debt" (notes
rows on the Assumption Statement.
Your Minimum Cash Requirement Was $5,000
The Cash To Fund Your Venture Is:...... $4,390

Diagram 5-12

The Derivation of the Cash Flow's Components

The components of the retail store's cash flow are derived from
several sources. Some items come directly from the Assumptions
Statement. Others come from the Balance Sheet or Income Statement. Again, the source statement is shown in parentheses.

Operating Cash Inflows

A/R collected from 1987 Sales

A/R collected from 1987 Sales are taken directly from the
amounts estimated in the Assumptions Statement.

Monthly Sales Collected

Monthly Sales Collected from 1988 Sales are calculated from the
sum of the following:

a) *Receivables Collected 30 Days After* Sale which is derived by multiplying the previous month's Net Sales (Income Statement) by the
assumed Percentage Collected in 30 Days (Assumptions
Statement).

b) *Receivables Collected 60 Days After* Sale which is derived by multiplying the Net Sales (Income Statement) that was realized two
months ago by the assumed Percentage Collected in 60 Days (Assumptions Statement).

c) *Receivables Collected 90 Days After* Sale which is derived by
multiplying the Net Sales (Income Statement) that was realized 3
months ago by the assumed Percentage Collected in 90 Days (Assumptions Statement).

d) *Receivables Collected Over 90 Days After* Sale which is derived by
multiplying the Net Sales (Income Statement) that was realized
4 months ago by the assumed Percentage Collected after 90 Days
(Assumptions Statement). Note: In this set of projections, Bad
Debts are part of Deductions and subtracted from Gross Sales.
An alternative calculation would be to make Receivables Collected add up to something less than 100% in the Assumptions
Statement with Receivables Collected Over 90 Days incorporat-
ing the shortfall (e.g., a cumulative Receivables Collected percentage of 98% equals a 2% Bad Debt Rate).

In some instances, cash sales are assumed to be any sale where
cash is received within the first 1 to 30 days. When this assumption
is made, cash sales are simply combined with Receivables Collected
instead of being listed as a separate item.

Diagram 5-13 shows how receivables are spread over time.

Accounts Receivable Spreading   DIAGRAM 5-13

	Actual		Projected					
Month	F	M	A	M	J	J	A	S
Sales	300	200	100	100	200	300	400	400
Cash Receipts								
1-30 days (20%)	60	40	20	20	40	60	80	80
31-60 days (50%)	150	150	100	50	50	100	150	200
61-90 days (30%)	120	90	90	60	30	30	60	90
Total Receipts From Sales	330	280	210	130	120	190	290	370

Adapted from Leon's Haller's excellent book, Making Sense of Accounting Information, Van Nostrand Reinhold, New York, 1985, p. 41 (with the author's permission).

Operating Cash Outflows

Payroll Paid
Payroll Paid is taken from Payroll, Taxes and Benefits (Income Statement).

Accounts Payable Paid
Accounts Payable Paid (from 1987 Expenses) is calculated by multiplying the 1987 Payables of $32,456 (Base Period of Balance Sheet) by the Initial A/P Balance % Collected/Month (Assumptions Statement).

Monthly Expenses, Inventory, Fixed Assets Paid
Monthly Expenses, Inventory, Fixed Assets Paid is calculated by multiplying Operating Expenses (Income Statement) minus Salaries and Wages and Depreciation plus Inventory Purchases (Inventory Purchases Statement) and Fixed Assets Purchased (Assumptions Statement) by a Percentage Paid Rate spread over 90+ days.

Vendor Deposits

Vendor Deposits is taken from Vendor Deposits Required (Assumptions Statement).

Interest on Debt (Notes Payable)

Interest on Debt (Notes Payable) is calculated by multiplying the Beginning Principal Balance (Cash Flow Statement) times the Annual Interest Rate (Assumptions Statement) and divided by 12 months.

Principal Payment

Principal Payment is calculated by subtracting the Interest on Debt (Notes Payable) from the Monthly Note Payment Amount (Cash Flow Statement).

Interest on Line of Credit

Interest on Line of Credit is calculated by multiplying the previous period's Line of Credit (Balance Sheet) times the Line of Credit Interest Rate (Assumptions Statement) and dividing by 12 months.

Add: Beginning of Month Cash Balance

Add: Beginning of Month Cash Balance is taken from the previous period's Cash and equivalents (Balance Sheet).

Line of Credit Principal Payments

Line of Credit Principal Payments occur when the Cash Balance Before Funding (Cash Flow Statement) plus new equity (Assumption Statement plus new debt (Assumption Statement) is above the $5,000 Minimum Cash Balance (Assumptions Statement). The exact amount paid is either the total principal due on Line of Credit Borrowings or the maximum amount that will still leave an Ending Cash Balance of $5,000.

New Equity

New Equity is taken directly from New Equity (Assumptions Statement) and is held at zero initially in order to determine incremental cash needs.

New Debt

New Debt is taken directly from New Debt (Assumptions Statement) and is held at zero initially in order to determine incremental cash needs.

Line of Credit Borrowings

Line of Credit Borrowings are calculated when the Cash Balance Before Funding plus New Equity and New Debt are less than the $5,000 Minimum Cash Balance (Assumptions Statement). The amount calculated is whatever amount is needed to make the Ending Cash Balance $5,000 without exceeding the Maximum Line of Credit (Assumptions Statement) of $50,000.

Our Ultimate Goal: Positive "Operating" Cash Flows

If happiness is a positive cash flow, then venture ecstasy is a positive OPERATING cash flow. One can finance a venture forever, show a positive cash flow by injecting new debt or equity, and never be profitable in either an accounting or economic sense.

Under certain conditions, a conscious decision may be made to subsidize a venture (e.g., some "non-profit" ventures) through donations and other fund raising activities. For instance, many symphonies and museums operate on this basis in order to keep admission prices affordable. Although they operate "in the red" every year, a positive cash flow is produced by annual gift giving or periodic capital campaigns.

Profit making ventures can use the same financial strategy if investors or bankers decide to buttress the venture indefinitely, often for very good reasons. I know of one venture that is extremely important to a semi-rural area in terms of jobs. The local bank, without taking any personal guarantees, supported the venture for many years, while the venture showed a negative operating cash flow, in order to maintain employment. Eventually the bank became dependent on the venture: if it went under, the bank would have gone with it. In another instance, a large-scale venture has yet to turn a positive operating cash flow or a profit for nearly ten years. Moreover, it's very likely *never* to do so! Nevertheless, loyal investors continue to support the enterprise for two reasons: they have an almost zealous attachment to the venture's mission which is so noble that additional infusions of equity are viewed as philanthropic gifts; and the non-cash flow benefits derived from prestige and networking provide a sustainable "non-economic" return to the investors.

Most ventures, however, do not fit these "non-profitmaking" profiles. The goal of most entrepreneurs, though it may be unappreciated and unstated, is to earn a positive *operating* cash flow.

Only as these operating cash flows increase over time can true wealth be created and equity increased in a venture, so that the value of the venture is worth something substantial to you because others place this value on it.

Creating this value means creating positive operating cash flows, and entrepreneurs must make a great many sound venture decisions to produce positive operating cash flows.

Summary: Appreciating the Linkages

In this chapter, we've seen how the initial assumptions you make will produce an interrelated set of projections. These projections start with a Revenue Statement and culminate in a Cash Flow Statement. Don't worry if you don't understand every interrelationship perfectly at this time. With experience, these linkages will become clearer. For now, it's enough to understand how every element of your financial projections are related to all other elements. There's a saying in business that a change in any part of an organization finds a way eventually of rippling across the entire venture. Your financial projections are no different.

Endnotes

1   "Mastering The Numbers'" Paul Hawken, *Inc. Magazine,* October, 1987, p. 19.

2   Dr. Who is a public television character who stars in a series bearing his name.

3   See Chapter Five of my *Entrepreneurship: Text, Cases, & Notes,* specifically the discussion of high variable cost ventures versus high fixed cost ventures.

4   "The Best-Laid Plans," *Inc. Magazine,* February, 1987, p. 61.

5   See "Compaq's Gamble On An Advance Chip Pays Off," in The Executive Computer by Peter H. Lewis in *The New York Times,* Sunday, September 20, 1987, p. F-14

Changing Your Assumptions: Analyzing Your Financial Projections

6

6

The Seven Health Tools

Assumptions are the driving force that produce your financial projections and, ultimately, your financial strategy. But how do you know if you should change your original assumptions once you've produced a set of financial projections? One way is to obtain new information from some source that causes you to make a change in your original thinking. For instance, you may do some research on your own or get new estimates from others with more experience that causes you to revise your assumptions.

Another way is to analyze the financial projections themselves using a variety of "health tools" to see if the projections meet certain standard benchmarks. The seven "venture health tools" are:

- Percentage Measures
- Profitability Measures
- Liquidity Measures
- Asset Productivity Measures
- Efficiency Measures
- Contribution Measures
- Breakeven Measures

However, interpreting the results generated by these health tools to see if they conform to certain benchmarks requires some judgement about how well the standards relate to your specific situation. As we shall see, the "rules of thumb" are far from absolute, especially for new ventures still in the Prestartup or Startup phases. You cannot apply the health tools nor use their results indiscriminately. Nevertheless, there are times when it is proper and profitable to use these health tools to evaluate your projections and to help you determine if changing your assumptions is necessary and/or possible.

Which Measures Are Relevant?

For both planned and existing ventures, a large and potentially unlimited number of measures can be constructed by combining different items drawn from your financial projections, your venture's actual performance, and/or other "non-financial" information (e.g., number of employees, number of actual workdays, etc.). Some of this non-financial information may not be unique to your industry *per se*. Some may be unique, and according to industry convention, considered very important. Some examples of these industry-specific measures are shown in the following table.

Examples of Industry-Specific Measures

Industry	Special Measures
Airlines	Available Seat Miles
	Revenue Passenger Miles
General Merchandise Store	Contribution Per Square Foot
Men's Hair Replacement	Advertising Dollars Per Lead
Service	Advertising Dollars Per Customer
Restaurant	Average Check Per Customer

I want to emphasize that these industry-specific measures are often incredibly important even though their number and diversity make them impossible to cover in this book. In fact, a similar statement can be made for a variety of measures that are "common" across industries. Percentages alone have an unlimited number of possibilities.

Because the measurement possibilities are so large, I will review a sample of measures which represent seven different ways to analyze your venture's planned or actual performance. Each of these can help you to decide whether you need to change your assumptions.

All seven are used as *comparative tools*. The comparisons fall into two categories:

1   Comparisons of your venture's performance for different time periods, e.g., is your venture performing better now compared to its earlier performance in terms of percentage performance, profitability, liquidity, etc.? How does current performance compare to future projected performance in terms of asset productivity, sales efficiency, contribution dollars, or breakeven?

2   Comparison of your venture's performance to other ventures, e.g., is your venture performing better now compared to other ventures in terms of percentage margins, profitability, etc.?

Both kinds of comparisons allow you to see trends (or lack of trends). Is profitability growing from one time period to the next? Are your sales per employee considerably different than the other ventures in your industry? While no single measure or comparison may be a sufficient indicator of health, the measures usually do give a reliable indication of health when:

■   they are evaluated as a group

- the measures are derived from projections that cover a sufficient period of time so that it can be assumed the venture has reached a level of financial stability (12 months of positive operating cash flow) usually associated with the post-startup phase.

The latter qualification is particularly true for the first five sets of measures since comparative benchmarks are drawn from data based on larger, established companies. For instance, the benchmark values for financial ratios, profitability measures, percentage comparisons, etc. are based on operating data for ongoing enterprises. 1 Unfortunately, as Diagram 6-1 illustrates, the measures have little relevance for new ventures when the data being analyzed cover the Prestartup phase and/or the early months of the Startup phase. I should stress two points here:

Relevance of Key Measures   *DIAGRAM 6-1*

Very Limited Relevance   Limited Relevance   Relevant
                                               But Care Needed in Interpreting Industry Comparisons   Relevant

< 1 Year   > 1 Year

PreStartup   Startup Phase   Post Startup

- The measures themselves aren't necessarily irrelevant, we just don't have enough knowledge about what the benchmark standards should be during these phases.
- You can still do projections during the Prestartup or Startup phases and use the health tools to analyze data extending a year or beyond the startup period. It is only the operating data or projections for these earlier periods that's difficult to interpret.

Because the potential number of key measures is quite large, very few analysts, even in the largest organizations, consider all of them. For instance, over thirty measures are identified in this chapter. In any given situation, any one of them can be important. They can also be meaningless, especially for new ventures. But, one thing is for certain few of us will use all of them. In fact, students, managers, and entrepreneurs often ask which ratios and other key measures they should focus on? That's a good question. Depending on your situation some key measures are more important than others. My position is that your specific situation is defined by three factors:

Your venture goals:
> For instance, Lifestyle Ventures don't need to focus on all the measures that are important to High Growth Ventures.

Your venture's maturity:
> Many measures are irrelevant during the Prestartup and Startup Periods.

Your industry:
> Certain measures are unique to an industry or simply more important.

Also, you may find the key measures you use to develop and manage your financial strategy can change as your venture goals change, your venture matures, and/or your industry orientation shifts. In my opinion, the number of measures that have real meaning and interest vary considerably between a solo entrepreneur running a Lifestyle Venture with zero employees versus a team of entrepreneurs running a High Growth Venture. The Lifestyle entrepreneur will need to focus on only a few measures while the High Growth entrepreneurs need to be cognizant of many more. Diagram 6-2 illustrates this relationship which can change for any venture as its venture goal shifts over time.

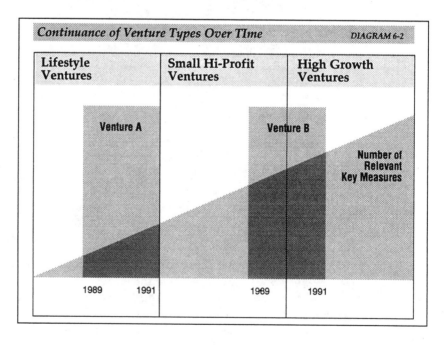

Continuance of Venture Types Over TIme   DIAGRAM 6-2

Some measures will also be more important than others to each entrepreneur. The measures that best reflect the hopes and aspirations of the venture will be particularly important. Diagram 6-3 shows the connection between your goals for the venture and the kinds of measures that relate directly to these goals. Diagram 6-4 represents my interpretation of which measures are the most relevant and practical for different kinds of ventures. The selection is "reality-based" in the sense that I realize that any or all of the measures can be important; however, experience has taught me that I and others only refer to a selection of them. For example, one end of the continuum is the solo entrepreneur who is running a Lifestyle Venture with no employees as a sideline venture. In this instance, one measure tends to be heavily used — Cash On Hand (i.e., your checkbook balance) — and, given the situation, it is the most relevant measure. But it isn't the only measure that should be considered. Diagram 6-4 attempts to go a step beyond to say what measures *should* be considered regularly by entrepreneurs in these different kinds of ventures.

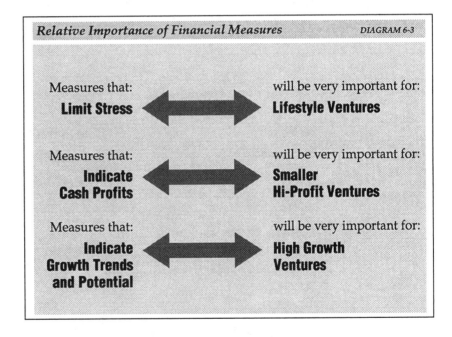

Relative Importance of Financial Measures   DIAGRAM 6-3

Measures that: → will be very important for:
Limit Stress **Lifestyle Ventures**

Measures that: → will be very important for:
Indicate Cash Profits **Smaller Hi-Profit Ventures**

Measures that: → will be very important for:
Indicate Growth Trends and Potential **High Growth Ventures**

Selected Financial Measures & Relative Importance   Diagram 6-4

For Three Kinds of Ventures with Particular Relevance For:

Key Measure	Lifestyle Venture	Smaller Hi-Profit Venture	High Growth Venture
1. Cash On Hand	X	X	X
2. Days Of Cash		X	X
3. Gross Margin	X	X	X
4. Operating Profit		X	X
5. Profit Before Tax	X	X	X
6. Profit After Tax		X	X
7. Return On Equity		X	X
8. Return On Investment			X
9. Return On Total Assets			X
10. Operating Profit To Net Worth		X	X
11. Working Capital			X
12. Current Ratio		X	X
13. Acid Test Ratio	X	X	X
14. Net Fixed Assets To Total Assets			X
15. Long Term Debt To Equity Ratio			X
16. Total Debt To Equity Ratio	X	X	X
17. Net Worth To Debt Ratio			X
18. Interest Coverage Ratio		X	X
19. Net Worth To Total Assets Ratio			X
20. Current Assets To Total Assets Ratio			X
21. Accounts Receivables Turnover (Days)	X	X	X
22. Inventory Turnover Ratio	X	X	X
23. Accounts Payable Turnover In Days	X	X	X
24. Total Assets To Net Sales($)			X
25. Fixed Assets To Net Sales($)			X
26. Net Sales To Working Capital ($)			X
27. Sales Per Day		X	X
28. Sales Per Employee		X	X
29. Contribution ($)		X	X
30. Contribution Margin ($)	X	X	X
31. Breakeven ($)	X	X	X
32. Breakeven Sales Price ($)		X	X
33. Industry-Specific Measures	X	X	X

At this point, let's briefly discuss each measure within the context of the seven health tools or seven kinds of analysis proven most useful when evaluating financial projections. I will note the basic idea behind each health tool, define which specific measures are most useful, and describe the key use(s) of each measure. 2

Venture Health Tool #1: Percentage Measures

The basic idea of percentage analysis is to convert absolute values to percentage values in order to get a better sense of certain relationships between the numbers. For the Revenue Statement and Income Statement, the various line items are taken usually as a percent of Net Sales. For the Balance Sheet, the usual procedure is to take the various assets, liabilities, and equities as a percent of Total Assets.

Which percentages are particularly useful? Important differences exist across industries about which percentages are the most insightful. But generally speaking, most entrepreneurs are interested in their gross margin (i.e., gross profit as a percentage of total sales), the percentages for selected operating expenses, and net profit margin. On the Balance Sheet, the percentage share of Current Assets and Fixed Assets as a percent of Total Assets is often insightful when compared to industry norms.

Percentage Analysis tells you which items are important and need backup budgets and schedules

Key Use: Percentages let you know which line items are large and important relative to other items in your financial projections. For instance, my reaction to R&D expenditures differs greatly if I see that they represent less than 1% for a venture versus 12% in another. In the latter case, the 12% tells me I probably need to carefully project this expense item and should support my figure with a budget. It also tells me where I and/or a senior R&D manager will need to spend our (future) time managing and monitoring these expenditures.

Percentages are also used as a means of comparing items across time periods to observe trends. You can also compare your venture's percentage performance with other ventures in your industry to see to what extent you are "in sync" with these industry averages. *Again, a word of caution for startups about percentage and ratio analysis is in order.* Percentages are useful as a comparative tool; but compared to what? Existing industry norms are usually available only for established firms. We have no truly good "industry statistics" for new ventures. Even worse, the percentages and ratios for existing industries usually include the losers (those ventures operating at a loss) along with the profitable concerns. As such, they represent an average that includes losers. 3 In terms of venture planning, your intent is to be neither "average" nor a "loser."

What can you do to get meaningful comparisons? As you do your field research on competitors or other comparable ventures in your industry, it will pay you to begin collecting information about their financial performances during their first five years, especially their first full year of operations. If you can obtain it, this information will give you a better indication of feasible percentages and ratios for comparison.

Finally, I should note that the percentages and ratios you generate for the first few months of your venture may have limited use, depending on the length of the startup period. For ventures that mature rapidly, the first few months may produce meaningful percentages. However, most ventures need more time to stabilize and for them, it makes sense to look only at the annual figures for most percentages.

Venture Health Tool #2: Profitability Measures

How profitable is your venture? To answer this question, you must do more than look at Net Profits on the Income Statement. A venture that has invested $1 million and, after ten years, is earning only $1,000 in annual Net Profits is hardly very profitable. A better way to express the question is, How profitably are the assets being used in this venture? Posed this way, we can see that measures of profitability must include one or more numbers from the Balance Sheet.

Profitability has meaning only when related to the amount of assets used to produce the profits

Four useful profitability measures and their uses are:
- Return On Equity (ROE)
- Return On Investment (ROI)
- Return On Total Assets (ROA)
- Return Of Operating Profit On Equity (Operating Profit To Net Worth Ratio)

Let me define each of these measures and provide some information about why they are used and what they mean.

Return On Equity

Return On Equity is calculated by dividing net income by total equity.

$$ROE = \frac{\text{Net Income}}{\text{Total Equity}}$$

*Key Use: Th*is measure is considered one of the most important measures of profitability. It tells us how profitable our venture is in terms of our total capital contributions plus capital we've reinvested in the venture as accumulated in retained earnings. Of course, you need to be certain all income and all equity are included in the calculation. In very small and newer ventures net income may have been minimized through a variety of perks and other maneuvers for tax or other reasons.

Returns on equity above 10% are usually considered good by many professional investors while returns from 15% to 20% are considered excellent for most established firms. Most professional investors, however, seek much higher returns for new ventures to account for the higher risks involved. These returns often range from 25% to 60% depending on when the investment occurs. For instance, "pure seed money" invested during the Idea or Venture Development Phase will require the higher returns.

Return On Total Investment

Return On Total Investment is calculated by dividing net income by [loans payable + long term loans payable + total equity]

$$ROI = \frac{Net\ Income}{All\ Debt + Equity}$$

Key Use: This measure tells us how much your venture earned on all the dollars invested in it, whether they be debt dollars or equity dollars. An increase in ROI over time is considered favorable to both equity and debt investors.

Return On Total Assets

Return On Total Assets is calculated by dividing net income by total assets.

$$ROA = \frac{Net\ Income}{Total\ Assets}$$

Key Use: Profit margins can be increasing but profitability can still be poor because total assets are excessive. The return on total assets is an excellent measure of overall profitability.

Operating Profit To Net Worth Ratio

Operating Profit To Net Worth Ratio is calculated by dividing operating profit by total equity.

$$OPNW = \frac{Operating\ Profit}{Total\ Equity}$$

Key Use: Tax and financial impacts can distort the profitability of venture "operations." This ratio tells us the venture's profitability from continuing operations before interest and taxes for each dollar of equity invested by the owners.

Venture Health Tool #3: Liquidity Measures

Bankers and others often want to know, "how liquid" is your venture? This question refers not only to the amount of cash on hand but also to the amount of current assets that are available for the venture's operations over the short term (i.e., the next 12 months or less). However, we can't just look at Cash, Accounts Receivables, Inventory, and Other Current Assets to determine the venture's liquidity. We have the same problem we had with trying to assess profitability by just looking at Net Profits. The problem is solved by comparing certain current assets to current liabilities. If we have a lot of Cash, Accounts Receivables, Inventory, and Other Current Assets *compared to* Total Current Liabilities, then we are very liquid. If we have more Current Liabilities than Current Assets, then the venture is not liquid.

How much liquidity is appropriate for a venture is a question that can be debated until the cows come home. Those entrepreneurs who still remember the Depression will tell you a long term view demands high, above average liquidity. A rainy day will come that will sway industry averages or rules of thumb about liquidity.

Other entrepreneurs and financial experts contend, however, that too much liquidity represents an inefficient use of resources. These "overly liquid" firms generally have lots of excess cash in bank accounts or marketable securities that could be earning much higher rates of returns. I have no definitive answer regarding this debate. I can give you the "Rules of Thumb," but from there the right decision is a matter of judgement about unique situations and circumstances, e.g., what other opportunities for investment are available; how long term is your view of your venture ... a few months, years, or decades until final disposition; what is the volatility of your industry; how recession/depression proof is your particular venture; etc.

Three measures of liquidity are defined below. The first two, Working Capital and the Current Ratio, are different expressions of the same things. In the former, a dollar number is produced by subtracting Current Liabilities from Current Assets. In the latter, a number is produced by dividing Current Assets by Current Liabilities. The Acid Test (or Quick) Ratio is a more conservative measure that considers only those current assets that are cash or readily converted into cash. The rationale is that during an emergency a venture should be able to cover all its current liabilities on short notice as an "Acid Test" of its liquidity.

Working Capital

Working Capital is calculated by subtracting total current liabilities from total current assets.

WC = CA - CL
General Rule: should be positive and growing

Key Use: A healthy venture should have positive working capital (i.e., current assets should exceed current liabilities). There are two reasons:

1   you should not use long term money to pay for short term obligations.

2   you want to have something left over to pay for expansion. Positive working capital means current assets are already available to pay for new obligations incurred from growth.

Current Ratio

Current Ratio = total current assets divided by total current liabilities

CR = CA / CL
General Rule: should be at least 2:1

Key Use: Many analysts feel it is too difficult to judge a venture's liquidity by just looking at a total dollar figure. Instead, they want to know how many dollars of current assets exist compared to current liabilities. Once a venture is relatively stable, the consensus is that a healthy liquidity position is one that sees at least $2 dollars of current assets for every $1 of current liabilities. There are, of course, exceptions to this rule. One of them is startups, especially startups during the Prestartup period.

First, let me say that the Current Ratio is very relevant for projections that cover several years after startup. Twelve to eighteen months after startup you should be looking for a liquidity position that shows $2 to $3 of current assets for every $1 of current liabilities — or else be able to explain the exceptions. However, during the prestartup period, the Current Ratio will have limited use for most ventures because there won't be any accounts receivable nor inventory (until just prior to startup). The magnitude of your Current Ratio under these conditions will be determined largely by your cash position and how close or far you are to your next financing milestone. The Current Ratio should be quite large just after a financing round, reflecting your cash rich position — a position you will quickly erode as you spend funds to reach another milestone. As you approach a new milestone, your Current Ratio should probably not slip under 1. In fact, as it approaches 1, the tendency is to cut back on incurring liabilities which often lengthens the Prestartup period. [4]

Acid Test Ratio

Acid Test Ratio equals cash plus accounts receivable plus any other ready cash assets e.g., marketable services divided by current liabilities.

ATR = [CASH + AR] / CL
General Rule: should be at least 1:1

Key Use: This measure is used to assess the solvency of a venture in terms of its ability to:

- respond to a crisis.
- take advantage of sudden opportunities that require cash.

The consensus is that *at least* $1 dollar of cash and other assets quickly converted into cash should be available to cover each $1 of current liabilities. My feeling is that the Acid Test Ratio should be considerably higher for new ventures just entering the startup period or for existing ventures making major expansions. The uncertainties of these situations and the need for quick response to unforseen problems and opportunities requires greater liquidity.

Venture Health Tool #4: Asset Productivity Measures

A number of different asset and debt ratios are used that help tell us how productive our assets are employed.

Several of these measures focus on the relationship between assets, debt, and equity. Others, called Turnover Ratios, focus on how quickly your venture is using different kinds of assets and liabilities.

The basic notion behind Asset and Debt Ratios is to see if a venture is properly capitalized given the relationship between assets, between assets and debt, and between the interest generated by the debt versus projected profits.

Net Fixed Assets To Total Assets Ratio

Net Fixed Assets To Total Assets Ratio is calculated by dividing (fixed assets - accumulated depreciation by total assets).

Ratio = Net Fixed Assets/Total Assets

Key Use: This measure tells us what portion of total assets are considered fixed assets. The size of this ratio is dependent upon the extent to which capital (fixed) assets are required by the business.

Long Term Debt To Equity Ratio

Long Term Debt To Equity Ratio is calculated by dividing long term loans payable by total equity.

Ratio = Long Term Debt / Total Equity
General Rule: .5 : 1

Key Use: This ratio shows the extent to which the owners are committed to the business by comparing the amount invested by creditors to that invested by owners.

Net Worth To Debt Ratio

Net Worth To Debt Ratio is calculated by dividing total equity by loans payable + long term loans payable.

Ratio = Total Equity / (Loans Payable + Long Term Debt)

Key Use: This ratio is the inverse of the Debt/Equity ratio. It also compares the investment of creditors to the investment of owners.

Interest Coverage Ratio

Interest Coverage Ratio is calculated by dividing operating profit by interest expense.

Ratio = Operating Profit / Interest
General Rule: 3 or 4 : 1

Key Use: This measures the extent to which the venture will be able to meet its required interest payments as they become due. There is a danger of default on loans outstanding when the interest coverage ratio is low or negative.

Net Worth To Total Assets Ratio

Net Worth To Total Assets Ratio is calculated by dividing total equity by total assets.

Ratio = Total Equity / Total Assets

Key Use: This ratio reflects the proportion of total assets provided by the venture's owners. A high ratio is desirable to potential creditors who see a good offer of the owners' investment to protect them against future losses.

Current Assets To Total Assets Ratio

Current Assets To Total Assets Ratio is calculated by dividing total current assets by total assets.

Ratio = Current Assets / Total Assets

Key Use: This reflects the portion of total assets that are comprised of current assets. If the ratio is too high, there may be problems with the way current assets are managed.

Turnover Ratios

How quickly we are using (turning over) certain assets and liabilities also gives us insight regarding their productivity.

|||||||||||||||| **NOTE** *Each turnover ratio is a weighted average of the sum of the balance sheet periods involved (i.e., 12 monthly or 4 quarterly periods) since the calculation usually is done on an annual basis.*

Cash Turnover In Days

Cash Turnover In Days is calculated by dividing cash by Net Sales * 365.

Days = [Cash / Net Sales] * 365

Key Use: This measure reflects the average number of days cash is available at the existing rate of operations. To be useful, the cash turnover should be examined in conjunction with other turnover ratios.

|||||||||||||||| **NOTE** *Sometimes it is useful to invert this formula to solve for cash if you assume you want a predetermined number of days of cash. (The same is true for the other turnover ratios.) Hence:*

Net Sales * (20 Days) = Cash Needed 365 Days

Accounts Receivable Turnover In Days

Accounts Receivable Turnover In Days is calculated by dividing accounts receivable by net sales * 365 days.

Days = (Accounts Receivable / Net Sales) * 365 days

Key Use: This ratio reflects the average number of days your customers take to pay the company. A high number of days might indicate a credit and/or collection problem.

Inventory Turnover

Inventory Turnover is calculated by dividing inventory by cost of sales.

Ratio = Inventory / Cost Of Sales

Key Use: Indicates the number of times the firm sold its inventory during the accounting period. In general, a high turnover rate indicates that inventory management is efficient.

Inventory Turnover In Days

Inventory Turnover In Days is calculated by dividing inventory by cost of sales * 365 days.

Days = Inventory / Cost Of Sales * 365 days

Key Use: This shows the average number of days of inventory the company has on hand. A high or rising number of days may indicate overstocking or inventory obsolescence.

Accounts Payable Turnover In Days

Accounts Payable Turnover In Days is calculated by dividing accounts payable by cost of sales * 365 days.

Days = Accounts Payable / Cost Of Sales * 365 days

Key Use: Shows the number of days the company is taking on average to pay its bills. The company's ability to pay its bills when due is influenced by the other turnover ratios we discussed.

Venture Health Tool #5: Efficiency Measures

How efficient are the assets being used? While asset profitability links assets to profits, asset efficiency ties certain assets to sales.

Sales Efficiency Measures are:

Total Assets To Net Sales

Total Assets To Net Sales is calculated by dividing total assets by net sales.

$ = Total Assets / Net Sales

Key Use: Provides a measure of how many assets in dollar terms are needed to generate an extra dollar of sales. Besides determining if the business activity is a low or high-fixed cost operation, you should also watch how this ratio changes over time to determine whether assets are being efficiently used.

Fixed Assets To Net Sales

Fixed Assets To Net Sales is calculated by dividing net fixed assets by net sales.

$ = Fixed Assets / Net Sales

Key Use: This measure shows how much fixed assets in dollar terms are needed to generate a dollar of sales. The trend of this ratio reflects the efficiency of fixed asset utilization to produce sales over time.

Net Sales To Working Capital

Net Sales To Working Capital is calculated by dividing net sales by (total current assets - total current liabilities).

$$\$ = \text{Net Sales} / (\text{Current Assets} - \text{Current Liabilities})$$

Key Use: Used to show how many sales dollars are generated per dollar of working capital. An upward trend in this ratio is considered favorable.

Sales Per Day

Sales Per Day is calculated by dividing net sales by number of days in period selected (i.e., 30, 90, or 365).

$$\$ = \text{Net Sales} / \text{Days}$$

Key Use: This measure reflects the average sales revenue per day within the accounting period. It's sobering sometimes to see the amount of sales you must generate daily to make sure you aren't kidding yourself about your ability to make your monthly or annual sales projections. For instance, a restaurateur may think he can do $1,000,000 in sales per year on a six day week, but dividing this amount by 312 days shows he needs to do $3,200.00 per day. This figure can be too high or too low depending on the venture's capacity (number of seats times average price per check).

The use of *sales per employee* and other similar measures are used the same way. Each industry has its own standards.

Venture Health Tool #6: Contribution Analysis

As a venture sells its products or services, some costs remain fixed over some range of sales volume while others vary with changes in sales. For several reasons, it helps to know which costs will vary with each sale versus those that will remain fixed over some relevant decisionmaking period (normally one year).

Those costs that are incurred only when you make a sale are 100% variable. Discounts, commissions, shipping and handling charges are examples of costs that are usually 100% variable costs. Once variable costs are identified, they are subtracted from total sales. The remainder is the "contribution to fixed costs and profits."

Total Sales - Variable Costs = Contribution to Cover Fixed Costs

Where "units" of production are defined, "unit contribution" is found simply by dividing total contribution by total unit output.

Key Uses: Why is it important to know the contribution for different products, services, or investment alternatives? The main reason is that it is possible to have high contribution products or services that provide low or no profit. Yet if one looks at profit alone, the temptation may be to de-emphasize or even drop low or negative profit products. Such action can inhibit a venture from covering its total costs since some of these costs are fixed and must be paid (e.g. rent, wages, salaries, advertising, etc.) no matter what you sell.

Also, contribution analysis helps us to compare one product versus another without being misled by historical allocations of overhead (i.e., fixed) costs. If we have to make a choice between Product A versus Product B because of limited resources, contribution measurement is one way to make the decision. For instance, we'd select Product A if its "Contribution per square foot" is higher than Product B, if limited shelf space only allowed us to sell one product.

Finally, from an entrepreneurial perspective, contribution analysis helps to do more than simply tell us which products or services will "contribute" the most to help cover fixed costs. It tells us how to allocate time during startup or during a venture crisis. Products that are high contributors help us to reach our breakeven sales faster.

Venture Health Tool #7: Breakeven Analysis

The distinction between fixed and variable costs also allows the calculation of breakeven points for single product businesses or, in more complicated cases, multiple product businesses. Breakeven analysis tells you how many units you must sell so that total revenues (net sales) will equal total costs. Diagram 6-5 graphs this relationship.

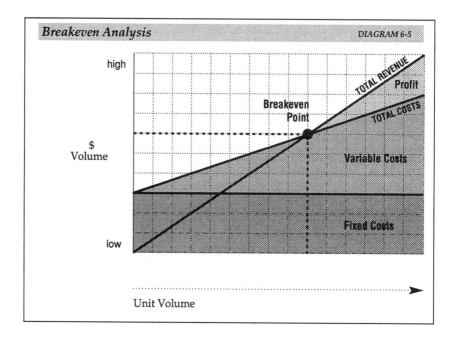

Breakeven Analysis   *DIAGRAM 6-5*

In order to calculate the breakeven volume (BEV), you must
know total fixed costs (FC) for a particular product plus the contribution per unit (CU) for the product. The contribution per unit also
equals the sales price (SP) per unit minus the variable cost per unit
(VC). Consequently, the formulas for breakeven analysis are:

$$BEV = \frac{FC}{CU} \quad \text{or}$$

$$BEV = \frac{FC}{SP\text{-}VC}$$

In some situations, you may not be given actual variable costs,
but only what variable costs are as a percentage of total sales. For instance, suppose you know fixed costs are $400,000 for a given level
of sales (100,000 units), and that variable costs are 70% of total sales.
Since contribution equals sales revenue minus variable costs, the contribution margin in percentage terms is simply:

Total Sales 100% - 70% = 30%.

To solve for breakeven sales:

$$BES = \frac{\$400,000}{1-.70} = \frac{400,000}{.30} = \$1,333,333$$

Basically, this breakeven calculation says we must sell more than
$1,333,333 to begin realizing a *profit*. Yet some organizations, espe-
cially small companies, may be interested in calculating the level of
sales needed to realize *a cash breakeven*. To calculate a cash
breakeven, you must determine which costs have not resulted in an

actual cash outflow (e.g., depreciation). For instance, if depreciation is $20,000, the procedure is to reduce fixed costs ($400,000) by $20,000. Consequently, cash breakeven is:

$$\text{CASH BES} = \frac{\$380,000}{.30} = \$1,266,666$$

Key Uses: Once you know breakeven sales, you can compare it with estimates of forecasted sales, total market size, your realistic share of market, and/or your available capacity. This allows you to answer questions such as: Do you have sufficient production capacity to attain breakeven volume? Is breakeven higher or lower than the share of market you can realistically hope to capture? Or, given the total market, what market share must you capture just to breakeven? Is the breakeven level of sales 40%, 60%, or 90% of forecasted sales? If it is 90%, how likely is it you will realize breakeven?

You will often be interested in calculating the breakeven sales price (BESP) given some desired unit output. For instance, an organization will not be able to operate higher than some level of unit capacity nor will it want to operate below some percentage of this capacity in order to avoid laying off people. The derivation of the breakeven sales price from equation No.2 above is:

BESP = (Fixed Costs /Number of Units) + Unit Variable Costs

$$\$13.33 = \frac{\$400,000}{100,000} + \$9.33$$

where

$$\$9.33 = \left(\frac{1,333,333 - 400,000}{100,000 \text{ units}} \right)$$

Ronstadt's FINANCIALS *and the Key Measures*

The thirty-plus ratios described in this chapter, plus other summary measures, are presented in a Key Measures Statement within Ronstadt's FINANCIALS. Every time you change your assumptions, the program recomputes the ratios and other measures for your new set of financial projections. Furthermore, it's easy to add new measures specific to your venture.

But, whatever the measures, the critical power of the program is the instantaneous tie between the Assumptions Statement and the Key Measures Statement. How valid are your assumptions? A quick look at the Key Measures Statement will often tell you if your assumptions are "in the ballpark." [5]

Summary: Drawing a Picture of Your Venture's Health

Once you develop a set of financial projections you need to ask: Overall, how financially healthy is my venture as represented by these projections? The next question is: What actions are appropriate given the venture's anticipated financial health as indicated by the financial projections?

These questions arm decision makers with a powerful capability to form a considered opinion about a prudent course of action. Is drastic action really necessary? After all, why perform surgery when a bandaid will suffice. Conversely, bandaids aren't much help if a venture needs open heart surgery to survive and prosper. These questions enable you to decide whether or not you should change your assumptions about your venture.

For unborn ventures, your financial projections (i.e., The Core Statements) are an important source of information for determining your venture's likely future health if you were to pursue a particular venture concept. For existing ventures, actual performance can be compared against earlier projections made for the same time period allowing you to ask: What differences exist between actual versus budgeted projections? What are the reasons for these differences?

The seven sets of measures discussed in this chapter are more than analytic or health tools *per se*. They are also reality checks or indicators that tell you if your original assumptions are realistic. For instance, you can complete your assumptions and generate a set of Core Statements; however, the results will be undesirable if:

- percentages are grossly inconsistent with the experience of comparable ventures.
- profitability and liquidity measures are weak.
- asset productivity and sales efficiency are poor.
- "contributions" are low while breakevens are high.

The issue, of course, is what do you do with this information. The answer is that you use the information to make decisions about the way you do business. These decisions may result in changes in your assumptions ... changes that alter your initial answers to the basic questions of Entrepreneurial Finance. The point is you just don't develop "a" set or "the" set of financial projections for your venture right off. Even if you are so fortunate, financial projections have a way of changing over time. The reality of financial decision making, at least good financial decisionmaking, is that you consider various options. Assumptions are altered. New assumptions are identified and tied into your financial calculations. "What if " scenarios are produced and refined. Eventually, you must identify the better financial alternatives.

Endnotes

1   The principal sources for industry and other comparisons of financial
    data are:

    Robert Morris Associates, *Annual Statement Studies*, 1616 Philadel-
    phia National Bank Building, Philadelphia, PA 1910

    Dun & Bradstreet's *Industry Norms and Key Business Ratios*, Dun &
    Bradstreet Corp., 299 Park Avenue, New York, NY 10171 (Annual).

    Troy, Leo, *Almanac Of Business And Industrial Financial Ratios*, Pren-
    tice Hall, Englewood Cliffs, NY (Annual).

2   Treatment of these different financial measures must be brief. Conse-
    quently, for those interested in learning more about each of these
    analytic tools, I suggest the following: Leopold A. Berstein, *Analysis
    Of Financial Statements,* Revised Edition, Dow Jones-Irwin, Homer-
    wood, IL, 1984.

    Leon Haller's *Making Sense Of Accounting Information,* Van Nostrand
    Reinhold, New York, 1985.

3   An exception is Troy, Leo, *Op. Cit.* Which excludes firms operating
    at a loss.

4   I'm speaking exclusively from experience. To the best of my
    knowledge, no one has researched the appropriate values for these
    and other ratios during the Prestartup period or, for that matter,
    during the Startup period.

5   The program contains an extensive glossary for each key measure in
    case, like me, you tend to forget the definition or implication of a cer-
    tain measure. All other statement terms are also included in the glos-
    sary and cross-referenced to related items. You need only place the
    computer's cursor on the item you don't understand and press a spe-
    cial help key.

How Much, When, and What Type of Money Does Your Venture Need?

7

7

Answering the First Three Key Questions

The preceding two chapters describe the basic components and analytic tools of financial projections. Chapters Seven through Ten describe how to use these components and tools to answer the five key questions of Entrepreneurial Finance.

This chapter answers three of these five questions for a single venture option. Specifically, the chapter addresses how much money is needed, when is it needed, and what type of money (debt or equity) is needed to cover Worst, Likely, and Best Case financial scenarios for a specific venture alternative. Chapter Eight expands this treatment by examining the venture alternatives that should be identified when starting or expanding a venture. Chapter Nine describes how to value one or more venture alternatives. Specifically, Chapter Nine asks how much is each venture alternative worth in terms of the equity you trade for the money your venture needs? Finally, Chapter Ten examines the dual question: Where should you seek the money your venture needs and what can you do to improve your chances of obtaining it?

How Much Money is Needed and When?

There are at least two factors that make answering these questions an ongoing and unique activity that's different for each venture.

One factor is time. The length of time to the next milestone affects the amount and timing of your venture's cash needs. Specifically where does your venture stands in the venture development process and how does this position affect your venture's value? Is your venture still an idea or has it already been launched? When is the next milestone that increases significantly the venture's valuation to the next group of investors? Unfortunately, the answers to these questions are unique for each venture. Diagram 7-1 illustrates key milestones for one software company. Several rounds of financing occurred in this case and at Point A (Idea) the relevant question was *not* how much money was needed to get to Point H (Follow-up Products), but how much was needed to get to Point B, then Point C, etc.

||||||||||||||| **NOTE**   *The logic for this procedure is covered in Chapter Two.*

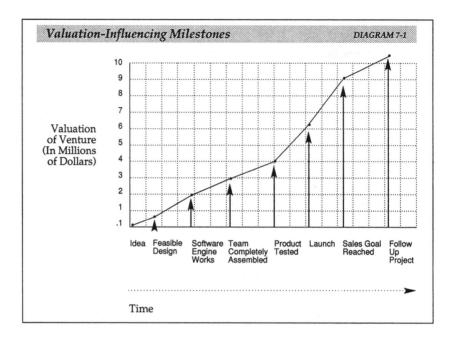

The second factor is the need to consider the extra cash needs to cover Worst or Best Case contingencies. In other words, you need to project your venture's cash needs to cover *a range of possibilities* because the cash needs for a Likely Scenario may not cover the cash needs for a Worst or Best Case Scenarios.

Taking these two factors into consideration, your overall objective is to: determine what amount of money is needed to reach the next "valuation influencing milestone" for the venture's Likely Scenario, as well as the increased cash needs (if any) required by the Worst or Best Case Scenarios (whichever is the larger).

For instance, assume the following funding requirements:

Likely Case = $500,000
Worst Case = $700,000
Best Case   = $750,000

Your funding needs are $750,000 ($500,000 for the Likely Case with contingency funds of $250,000 to cover the Best Case, since it is larger than the Worst Case Scenario). I should add that you should be aware of both numbers — the Likely Case dollar needs of $500,000 and the extra dollar needs of $250,000 due to the Best Case — even though your total funding needs are equal to the Best Case of $750,000. Since the Likely Case has (by definition) a higher chance of occurring, you want to be clear about the amount of funds you absolutely need (the Likely Case) plus the amount of contingency funds you need as a reserve fund.

The Cash Flow Statement tells you the magnitude of your capital needs and the timing of these needs based on the assumptions you make about your venture. For example, let's consider some variations in assumptions that produce different financial projections and cash needs for your fledgling Retail Store. Let's assume the financial projections presented in Chapter Five represent the Likely Scenario. In our Cash Flow Statement, "Additional Funding" (located near the bottom of the Statement) was purposely set at zero so we could see how much money was needed during the first twelve months of operations. This amount was revealed by the last item, Minimum Cash Balance. The figure shown was $84,341 (which is actually the $-79,341 Ending Cash Balance minus the additional $5,000 Minimum Cash Balance you require each month). The Ending Cash Balance for each month (reproduced here) told us *when* the funds would be needed (i.e., how much money was needed each month to yield a monthly Ending Cash Balance of zero dollars).

Date	Ending Cash Balances
1/31/88	$ -107
2/29/88	$-31,744
3/31/88	$-44,822
4/30/88	$-49,306
5/31/88	$-42,408
6/30/88	$-35,150
7/31/88	$-32,427
8/31/88	$-41,773
9/30/88	$-60,583
10/31/88	$-79,341
11/30/88	$-55,970
12/31/88	$-9,072

These numbers tell us:

- The month of October has your worst cumulative negative cash flow of $-79,341. Add to this figure the $5,000 you said you always want to have "on hand" and we get the Maximum Cash Required of $84,341;

- The negative cash flows decline dramatically in November and December. In fact, they had declined earlier during May, June, and July before the negative cash flows began building again through October. These declines are due to the positive *operating* cash flows projected during those same months of May, June, July, November, and December.

Armed with this cash flow information, you have the ability to focus on the adjustments that can be made to either limit these negative cash flows and/or finance them through debt and/or equity funds. Specifically, for the Likely Case of the venture concept being considered, you now have three basic options to change this Ending Cash Balance:

a) change one or more of the assumptions so that your cash flow position is improved;

b) add debt, equity, or some combination of the two; or

c) some combination of options a and b.

Before considering adding debt and/or equity, you should first review your assumptions and some of the analytic "health" measures covered in Chapter Six. This review is to see if it is *realistic* for you to change one or more assumptions so that the ultimate result is an improvement in your cash flow, thereby reducing the amount of money you need. However, you must be very cautious when making these changes, as I will explain in a moment. For now, you should know that the following changes generally have a positive impact on cash flow. The amount of cash your venture needs will *decrease* to the extent you can:

- Increase price and/or volume, (i.e., increase sales revenues).
- Reduce operating costs and expenses, (i.e. spend less on wages, marketing, production, etc.).
- Increase the rate at which you collect your Accounts Receivables (i.e. get people who purchased your product to pay you faster).
- Reduce the time a product spends in inventory (i.e., increase the speed that you use or "turnover" inventory, thereby decreasing the amount of time you have cash tied up in inventory).
- Reduce the amount and rate of cash expenditures on equipment, furniture, and other fixed assets.
- Increase the time you take to pay your Trade Payables.
- Increase the time you take to pay your Accrued Expenses.
- Reduce the amount and rate you pay back any other obligations.

Of course, you need to justify these changes on the basis that they are *possible* within the context of a Likely Case Scenario. Don't get mesmerized by computer numbers. Things won't really change just because you "will them to change." For instance, it may be impossible to change one or more assumptions without having a corresponding negative impact on cash flow. A price increase past a certain point will produce a decline in demand. Your customers may simply be unwilling to pay the higher price. The resulting reduction in volume may more than offset the dollar gains derived from lifting prices. Similarly, reducing costs may result in inefficiencies and the emergence of new costs when, for example, a lower paid workforce produces inferior products. Speeding up receivables collection may cause lost sales. Extending the time you take to pay vendors and others may result in higher charges or a need to deal with less reliable suppliers. Clearly, good information about your customers, suppliers, workforce, etc. is needed to determine how much the assumptions can be changed before negative effects swamp the positive effects.

Entrepreneurs need to develop skills to get cash to flow into a venture faster and to flow out slower. However, one can move prudently only so far in accelerating inflows and delaying outflows before the venture is adversely affected. Part of the entrepreneur's cash flow skill involves knowing just how far to go without jeopardizing the venture. Another part involves finding creative ways to accelerate the inflows and retard the outflows. And yet another part involves designing the venture initially in such a way that opportunities exist for maximizing cash inflows while minimizing the outflows.

For instance, the effect on the Retail Store's cash flow of changing the original assumptions can be seen below. Under the new assumptions, sales have been increased 10% to $330,000. Accounts Receivables (AR) collections have been speeded up so that 95% of all sales are collected within the first 30 days and the remaining 5% are now collected during the second month. By contrast, Accounts Payable (AP) are stretched so that 40% are paid during the first month, 30% during the second month, and 30% during the third month (versus 70% and 30% for the original assumptions). The result is a new set of Core Statements where the Cash Flow Statement shows a new Maximum Cash Required that is approximately $30,000 less than the cash required under our original set of assumptions.

	Original Assumptions	Revised Assumptions
Sales	$300,000	$330,000
% ARs First Month	80%	95%
% APs First Month	70%	40%
Maximum Cash Required	$ 84,341	$53,004

The Minimum Amount: Do not confuse the Maximum Cash Required with the timing question. The Maximum Cash Required is not the minimum amount you necessarily need at the start of the venture to produce a positive cash flow. In this instance, the maximum cash required is the amount you need to cover the largest negative cash flow in October. In fact, injecting the Maximum Cash Required into our venture during the first month can be too expensive (in interest payments if debt is used, or the amount of equity given up). The point is that a cushion is already being built into our Cash Flow if you assume the $84,341 is necessarily the amount of money your venture needs at startup. It is the correct amount if your Maximum Cash Required occurs in January. Otherwise, it may be an appropriate and timely amount (as it probably is in this instance), since you don't want "to cut it too close" regarding the infusion of funds. However, it can be the wrong amount, especially in larger ventures where the numbers are magnified.

To find the right amount you need to experiment phasing in various amounts of debt or equity money over time, to see when an acceptable Ending Cash Balance is produced. The same process has to be repeated for the Best and Worst Cases so we can see what "contingency funds" are needed should these scenarios occur.

The example below is a simple one but effectively illustrates this process. It shows the Maximum Cash Required (drawn from the respective cash flow statements) for an assumed Worst and Best Scenario. The first row of cash needs assumes only a change in your store's sales level. A drop in sales from $300,000 to $200,000 increases cash needs to $92,562. At the same time, the cash needs for the Best Case drops to $76,120. It may be possible to realize sales of $400,000 without an increase in costs. However, sales increases often mean increases in the costs of doing business. Consequently, *the $76,120 can be unrealistic because the assumptions underlying* the number are unrealistic. In fact, we can see that our Maximum Cash Required grows to $105,957 for the Best Scenario when *we assume* increases are needed in advertising and inventory to generate the $400,000 in sales.

Retail Store: Maximum Cash Required

	Worst	Likely	Best
1. Sales Level	$200,000	$300,000	$ 400,000
2. Cash Needs For Sales ChangeOnly	$ 92,562	$ 84,341	$ 76,120
3. Cash Needs For Sales AndOtherChanges	$ 92,562a	$ 84,341a	$105,957[*b]

a) no changes assumed

*b) changes include more advertising (6% versus 3%) and more inventory that requires slightly longer lead time for purchasing (3monthsversus2months)

The implication of this example is that we need at least $84,341 with access to an additional $22,000 ($105,957 - $84,341) to cover the larger (Best Case) situation. These amounts assume we can only "go to the well" once and that equity funds are used.

What Type of Money Does Your Venture Need?

How much money is needed and when it's needed also influences whether you choose to employ equity or debt funds.

IIIIIIIIIIIII **NOTE** *My purpose here is to illustrate the direct cash flow implications of debt versus equity, as opposed to the strategic and financial considerations associated with this decision, as discussed in Chapter Two.*

From a cash flow perspective, remember, debt funds create immediate cash outflows of interest payments and possibly principal payments. Equity funds nearly always assume no dividend outflows or repayments of capital until the venture is firmly established or harvested in some way.

Our Retail Store's Cash Flow told us how much money we needed and approximately when these funds are needed. Next, to see the effects of using debt or equity, you need to experiment with different combinations of debt and/or equity to see their impact on your *operating* cash flow, not just your ending cash flow. Remember, you need to ask how a positive Ending Cash Flow is being produced. Is it from operations or is it from additional financing? Does one level and mix of financing produce a positive *operating* cash flow appreciably faster than another while minimizing the amount of equity you must give up?

For example, let's assume you can raise your Likely Case needs of $84,341 in equity. You also have the possibility of raising less equity funds and combining them with debt. What should you do?

First, if all debt is used, you will need more than $84,341 since some of this money will be needed to pay the interest (assumed at 11.5% annually in this example) on this borrowed money. How much more and what impact the interest expense will have on your Income Statement can be seen by creating "All Equity" versus "Equity & Debt" versus "All Debt" scenarios. The debt/equity combination assumed $50,000 in equity and $40,000 in debt. The totals of $90,000 (Debt/Equity) and $110,000 (All Debt) were the amounts needed to produce positive Ending Cash Balances with a Minimum Cash Balance of approximately $5,000. The following outcome for Net Profit was produced on the respective Income Statements for each scenario.

Income Statement

	All Equity Scenario ($84,341)	Equity & Debt Scenario ($90,000)	All Debt Scenario ($110,000)
	highest	next highest	lowest
Net Profit Before Tax	$41,502	$39,222	$34,093

An important issue, of course, is how much equity you must give up to earn the higher Net Profit under the All Equity or Partial Equity options. If you must give up considerable equity, the use of some or all debt becomes increasingly attractive. However, as you consider debt options, you need to be certain that there is sufficient cash flow to cover "priority" or "must pay" items. Both principal and interest payments will increase the amount of priority outflows. To what extent does this increase limit your ability to cover other items of lower priority that nevertheless may still be very important? For instance, the amount of principal and interest payments for our Retail Store increase from $600 per month at the beginning of the year to over $1,600 by the end of the year as more debt is used. Total principal and interest payments for the year are $15,000. This is money that can be used to expand the venture if an all-equity approach is available and used.

Of course, what type of money you employ is not decided solely on cash flow considerations. As discussed in Chapter Two, there are ownership considerations and personal risk considerations that may make the cash flow impacts less important. In one instance, equity may simply not be a viable option; in another situation, it may be the only possibility.

Getting More Refined: How Budgets and Schedules Help You to Determine How Much Money is Needed and When

Developing selected budgets and schedules is one way to get a better feel for the validity of your assumptions about how much money you need and when you need it. A budget is a detailed list of sales, costs, and/or other expenditures covering some period of time. For example, a monthly R&D Budget identifies individual research and development expenditures by month; an annual Manpower Budget breaks down the number of people working for your venture by position over the next year; a quarterly Sales Budget lists sales by product or other categories into three month groupings. These budgets are often called "line item budgets."

A schedule serves a similar purpose and sometimes the term is used interchangeably with budget. In this book, the term "schedule" is used to describe a list of expenditures that represents an additional breakdown of a budget item or one that may cut across more than one budgetary area; e.g., a schedule of equipment, a schedule of supplies, or a schedule of office furniture.

Budgets and schedules are useful because their development often provides you with a more realistic and accurate estimate of the line items in your projections. If you have a tendency to be overly optimistic, they help to check your tendencies to inflate sales and forget about certain costs.

Supporting Statements can also be used to clarify calculations that are otherwise hard to follow, especially for readers unfamiliar with your projections. For instance, the buildup of purchases for our

Retail Store is not easy to deduce from the Statements presented in Chapter Five. Consequently, a brief Supporting Schedule has been produced (See Diagram 7-2) that traces this calculation.

From a control perspective, budgets and schedules also let you see where changes might be made or have to be made, especially as you collect actual information about your operations. Actual versus budget comparisons are invaluable tools for venture decisionmaking.

When Should You Develop Supporting Budgets and Schedules?

Generally, you don't need detailed budgets and schedules during the "Concept Development Phase" (see Diagram 1 in the Preface); i.e., while you are developing a Venture Feasibility Plan. However, budgets and schedules are the basic building blocks for your financial projections in your Business Plan during the Venture Formation Phase. They are also fundamental tools for operating an ongoing enterprise during the Venture Renewal Phase. In fact, one reason some entrepreneurs find that their business and operating plans become obsolete quickly is that they lack the budgetary detail to make them accurate and usable documents in the first place. Their critical use is to help you refine your assessment of how much money is needed and when it's needed. Once you are seriously committed to a venture, it pays to start developing budgets and schedules for major line items.

Using Ronstadt's FINANCIALS to Produce Detailed Budgets

Ronstadt's FINANCIALS contains a tremendous budgeting feature. The program can create unlimited subrows that can be hidden or exposed below each row. At each level, the subrows will add up automatically to the parent row. This capability of having unlimited numbers of "nested rows" allows you to include a great deal of budgeting information in the Core Statements, information that can be hidden or exposed with a simple keystroke.

The example in Diagram 7-3 shows how these nested rows work. You can add an unlimited number of subrows to each row.

Supporting Statement: Inventory Purchases
Retail Company

	1/31/88 Retail	2/29/88 Retail	3/31/88 Retail	4/30/88 Retail	5/31/88 Retail	6/30/88 Retail	7/31/88 Retail	8/31/88 Retail	9/30/88 Retail	10/31/88 Retail	11/30/88 Retail	12/31/88 Retail	Year 1 Retail
Monthly Inventory Purchases													
Purchases store A.........	$11,025	$13,750	$12,150	$9,450	$6,750	$2,700	$5,400	$12,150	$27,000	$35,100	$5,940	$8,168	$149,583
Detail Of Monthly Purchases													
Store A purchases													
Based on lead-time.....	4,725	6,750	12,150	9,450	6,750	2,700	5,400	12,150	27,000	35,100	5,940	8,168	136,283
Add'l invty required ..	6,300	7,000	0	0	0	0	0	0	0	0	0	0	13,300
Total store purchases..	11,025	13,750	12,150	9,450	6,750	2,700	5,400	12,150	27,000	35,100	5,940	8,168	149,583

Diagram 7-2

Nested Rows At Work					Diagram 7-3
All Subrows Hidden		**Some Subrows Exposed**		**All Subrows Exposed**	
Net Sales	$100.00	Net Sales	$100.00	Net Sales	$100.00
Cost of Sales	$ 50.00	Cost of Sales	$ 50.00	Cost of Sales	$ 50.00
Gross Profit	$ 50.00	Gross Profit	$ 50.00	Gross Profit	$ 50.00
Operating Expenses	$ 45.00	Operating Expenses	$ 45.00	Operating Expenses	$ 45.00
		R&D	$ 5.00	R&D	$ 5.00
		Labor	$ 10.00	Labor	$ 10.00
		Marketing	$ 20.00	Marketing	
				Marketing Communications	$ 10.00
				Selling	$ 10.00
		G&A	$10.00	G&A	$ 10.00
Profit Before Tax	$ 5.00	Profit Before Tax	$ 5.00	Profit Before Tax	$ 5.00

While your capability to add subrows is unlimited, you should create additional supporting statements to show lengthy detail. Diagram 7-4 illustrates this process. Also, each row or subrow can be footnoted with up to 128 lines of assumptions, instructions, or general comments.

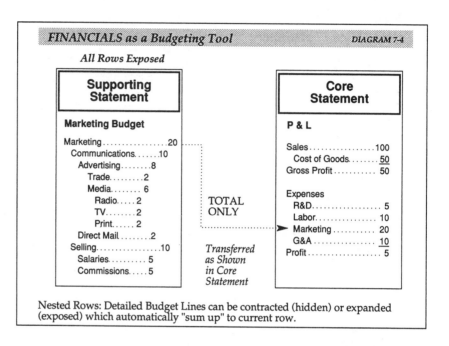

FINANCIALS as a Budgeting Tool   *DIAGRAM 7-4*

All Rows Exposed

Supporting Statement

Marketing Budget

Marketing................20	
Communications......10	
Advertising........8	
Trade........2	
Media........6	
Radio.....2	
TV........2	
Print......2	
Direct Mail........2	
Selling................10	
Salaries.........5	
Commissions.....5	

TOTAL ONLY

Transferred as Shown in Core Statement

Core Statement

P & L

Sales................100	
Cost of Goods.......50	
Gross Profit..........50	
Expenses	
R&D.................5	
Labor..............10	
➤ Marketing..........20	
G&A...............10	
Profit.................5	

Nested Rows: Detailed Budget Lines can be contracted (hidden) or expanded (exposed) which automatically "sum up" to current row.

Supporting Statements, whether they be budgets or schedules, are easy to create in Ronstadt's FINANCIALS. They are also easy to link with your Core Statements because they usually tie into only one line item. For instance, the Marketing Budget sums all subrows to Total Marketing Expenses ($20,000) which is copied or linked to Marketing Expenses in the Income Statement. Then, whenever you change a single number in your Marketing Budget, Ronstadt's FINANCIALS allows you to see its impact on all your financial projections.

Once a Likely Scenario is created, it is very easy to change assumptions, including budget assumptions, so that Worst and Best Case Scenarios are created as separate files. A unique capability of Ronstadt's FINANCIALS is its ability to bring these multiple scenarios into your computer's main memory (Random Access Memory) at the same time. In other words, you can compare the Likely, Best, and Worst Case Scenarios side-by-side. You can even graph selected items or print them. For instance, Diagram 7-5 graphs Net Sales for Worst, Likely, and Best Scenarios for your Retail Store.

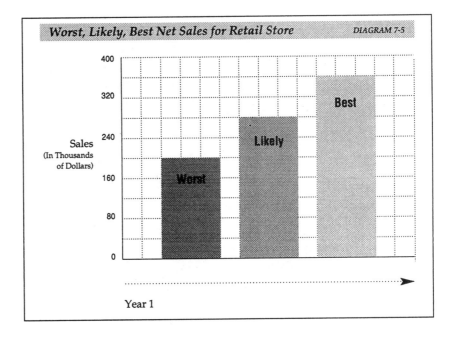

Another key feature is the program's ability to quickly alter the time periods being considered. For instance, experienced entrepreneurs will tell you it's common for the launch date to get pushed back. You think sales will start in January, but they don't get started until March. Similarly, you think monthly projections, particularly cash flows, are appropriate for the first twelve months. Later, a better understanding of your venture process indicates that monthly projections should be extended to fourteen, sixteen, eighteen, etc., months. Ronstadt's FINANCIALS can make both these changes in seconds, whereas conventional spreadsheets take hours, if not days, and open another opportunity for serious error.

Summary: Avoiding Serious Venture Pain

All the Core Statements can be used to assess the viability and potential future value of a venture. However, the Cash Flow Statement is the statement we use most frequently as a starting point for answering the first three questions of Entrepreneurial Finance:

- How much money does my venture need?
- When will my venture need this money?
- What type of money (debt or equity) should I use?

The truth of the matter is that these questions have been deceptively difficult to answer correctly in the past. This difficulty is the reason why more than a few entrepreneurs have skipped venture planning, at least financial venture planning. Their tendency has been to trust their instincts or intuition about cash flow rather than waste their time doing cash flows projections.

This intuitive approach has worked for some, especially when the venture fortuitously experiences good times. But my impression is that "intuitively gifted entrepreneurs" are few in number, despite the fact that some successful entrepreneurs like to talk about their "gut instinct." Entrepreneurial bravado aside, more often than not one finds upon closer inspection that the "keen intuition" of these entrepreneurs has been financed by giving up too much equity for the comfort of having a large cash position. It's a position that's easy to monitor while the venture realizes good growth and good margins. But as the October 1987 stock market crash revealed, many people can do well in a bull market — it's when the bears arrive that the wheat gets separated from the chaff. The same is true for the "intuitively gifted entrepreneur." Intuition has a way of evaporating when a venture experiences a major setback.

Moreover, most entrepreneurs — especially fledgling entrepreneurs — don't usually have to wait for a major setback before experiencing financial difficulties. Lacking a large financial cushion, they soon find themselves in a cash flow bind because they haven't done their homework about the cash needs of their business.

And homework is clearly required. The process of creating superior financials for venture planning purposes demands a serious effort, one that is commensurate with the risks of the venture you are contemplating. As a new entrepreneur, you will probably have a good share of your personal savings on the line. You may have remortgaged your home. Personal guarantees may have been signed for bank loans. Friends and relatives may have invested. Clearly, this is not the time to take foolish risks. Pushing numbers may be painful to you, but you better be ready to endure some slight discomfort. Otherwise, your "slight discomfort" may be quickly replaced by some serious venture pain.

There are ways, however, to make the experience of developing financial projections a rewarding one while limiting the pain most of us feel when required to work with numbers. The secret is having some clear objectives about what you want from your financial projections in the first place. The process becomes less torturous when your objectives become the objectives of Entrepreneurial Finance — to answer our "deceptively simple" questions: How much money does my venture need? When does my venture need this money? and, What type of money (debt or equity) does the venture need?

Which Venture Alternatives Should You Consider?

8

8

Venture Alternatives

Alternatives ... the identification and evaluation of viable alternatives are at the heart of all good decision making. Decision making itself means deciding among choices. But identifying the choices isn't always clear-cut nor obvious when it comes to creating a new venture or making major expansions and diversifications of an existing venture. What kinds of alternatives should you consider when starting or expanding a venture?

In practice, this decision usually becomes complicated, even mind-boggling, because each venture alternative can have any number of financial scenarios. After all, a financial scenario is simply a set of assumptions with particular values. Change any single value and a new scenario is created. Change the values past some critical point, or add new assumptions, or delete existing ones, and you have created a substantially different way to pursue a venture concept. Continue this process far enough and eventually you will even create a different venture concept.

In this chapter, I will present a simple procedure that will help you to identify a few key alternatives that represent the basic ways to conceive and implement your venture. For instance, you need to be explicit about your "Preferred Venture Concept" versus your "Least Cost Venture Concept" (i.e., the least cost way to start or expand your venture). You also need to identify these two venture concepts during the Venture Feasibility Phase. Assuming you move beyond this Phase and write an Operations Plan or Business Plan, the next step is to determine the preferred and minimum levels of resources you require for your Preferred Concept. You also should determine more exactly the financial resources you will need for your Least Cost Concept in case you do not receive *any* financing for your Preferred Concept. Diagram 8-1 illustrates this procedure.

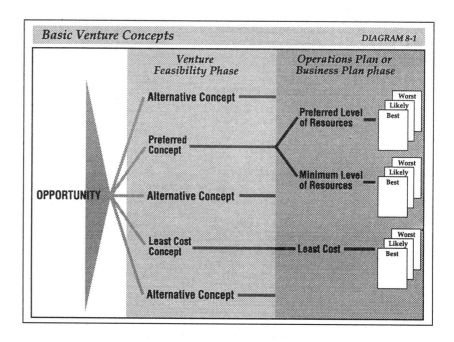

I should add at this point that you do *not* have to present all these venture options and their projections in your Operations Plan or Business Plan. But you do need to develop them ... just in case.

Concept Identification: Venture Feasibility Phase

There are usually many ways to create or expand a venture in terms of responding to a perceived customer opportunity. Furthermore, each particular venture concept has a Worst, Likely, and Best Case scenario. You generally cannot and should not analyze all the venture possibilities. For instance, in the *Venture Feasibility Phase,* you don't have the time nor information to look at Worst, Best, and Likely Cases for every way to assemble a venture. At best, you may have time to consider a very rough Likely Case for what turns out to be the two or three most promising ways to initiate your venture. (See Diagram 8-2)

But how do you identify, for example, the top three concepts? Perhaps the best way to give substance to these ideas is with a real example. For instance, a venture I'm intimately familiar with recently considered a major expansion (in effect a new venture) built around the software program, Ronstadt's FINANCIALS. The venture expansion was a response to a particular customer need (market opportunity) — specifically, the interrelated need of many groups for financial projections, budgeting, and a financial decision making capability. Of course, there were many possible ways to respond to this need. A large number of venture concepts existed just in terms of combinations of potential customer groups and potential product

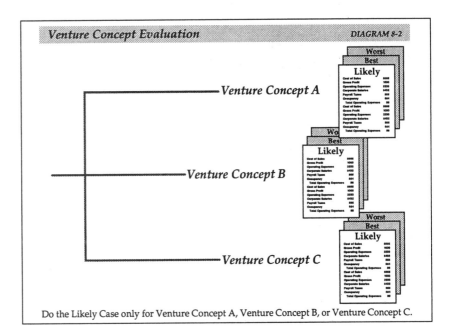

Do the Likely Case only for Venture Concept A, Venture Concept B, or Venture Concept C.

features and benefits. Diagram 8-3 summarizes only a few of these possibilities. The combinations were quite extensive because:

a) each of the customer groupings could be further subdivided or sequenced;

b) various product features could be combined to create a particular venture concept; and

c) various customer groups could be combined to create a venture concept.

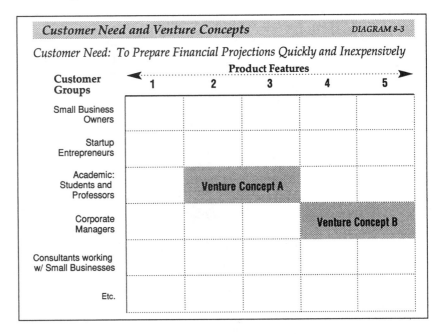

The combinations and alternatives you will face in your own venture will be just as numerous. Nevertheless, too many entrepreneurs fail to consider these possibilities. Instead, what you should do is use this customer/product information to list the venture concepts that seem remotely possible — no matter how wild or crazy they may seem. Defer being judgmental or critical until you feel you've exhausted the concept possibilities. My experience here is that most prospective entrepreneurs see only one or two concepts — when actually fifteen or twenty exist. Often, now's the time to bring in others to help you brainstorm different concept possibilities.

You may ask, "Isn't this make-work?" The answer is clearly "no" because a long line of research shows that a definite link exists between the *quantity* of creative ideas and the *quality* of these ideas and, furthermore, the better ideas are often the last ones — not the first ones you identify. 1

Next, don't just limit yourself to customer/product combinations. Ask yourself what different kind of businesses are possible. Do you want to be an R&D company, versus a company that focuses on the production of products or services, versus one concerned mainly with the marketing and selling of these products, or will your venture embody two or all three of these possibilities? Also, the marketing and production pathways to your customer(s) usually represent a different kind of business. For instance, the skills and resources to be a direct marketing company are considerably different from a marketing pathway that employs resellers. How you reach the end user often represents a distinctive venture concept. The same is true for production processes. The skills and resources needed to be a custom or specialized (job shop) producer are vastly different from those needed to be a batch producer, versus a mass producer, versus a subcontractor.

Once you've identified a number of venture concepts, the third step is to evaluate the concepts on qualitative grounds plus a few key numbers (likely price, margins, market size, and likely investment). One important question is which of these concepts represents the *least cost way* of getting into business that is acceptable to you. To be safe, you probably should include this concept with the two or three venture concepts that seem the best to you.

The *least cost way* is NOT the same as the answer to the question: "What venture concept can I use to pursue this opportunity with the maximum amount of resources I have available or can get?" This is because the maximum amount of resources you have available or can get may not be sufficient to fund any of the venture concepts identified in response to a perceived customer opportunity.

Your fourth step is to develop and refine your quantitative estimates by examining the Likely Case scenario for the two or three venture concepts to determine the *rough* level of resources you need to do the venture.

Scenario Identification:
The Operations or Business Plan Phase[2]

At the start of the operations or business planning phase, you need to continue working on your Preferred Venture Concept. Since some time will probably have passed since you did your venture feasibility, you should refine your Likely Case Scenario for your "Preferred level of resources." In addition, you need to develop the Worst and Best Cases for your Preferred concept in order to determine the amount of money you need to start the venture or move to your next major milestone.

Your next step is to identify and develop the Worst, Likely, Best Case for what you believe is the *minimum* level of resources that is acceptable to you for your Preferred Concept. The same process continues for your Least Cost Concept, as show in Diagram 8-4.

For financial or other personal reasons, you may decide that the Minimum Resource Option is the only one you wish to consider. However, my own experience indicates that there are many entrepreneurs who decide for good reasons that, *if they can raise the funds,* they and their venture will be better off if the Preferred Level Of Resources is pursued. Unfortunately, what then happens is that they soon forget about planning for the Minimum Level Of Resources, just in case they don't get the "preferred" level of funds.

I should stress that the option associated with the Minimum Level Of Resources sometimes represents a very different way to pursue your preferred venture concept because the cutbacks you need to make force you to do things in a fundamentally different way (compared to the option associated with your Preferred Level Of Resources). In these instances your Minimum Resource Option may represent a different approach to realizing your venture.

As shown in Diagram 8-4, the key difference is pursuing Venture Concept B by a heavy marketing investment in "going retail" versus a less expensive direct marketing program.

The Least Cost Concept represents another way to realize your venture opportunity, but is one that is fundamentally different from your Preferred Concept. It is important to realize that a substantial financial difference should exist between *the Minimum Level Of Resources for your Preferred Concept versus the resource requirements for your Least Cost Concept.* In fact, the Least Cost Concept should be easy to pursue, financially speaking, otherwise it probably won't be viable. Remember, the Least Cost Concept comes into play only after you've failed to raise the Minimum Level Of Resouces for your Preferred Concept. Unless a meaningful financial gap exists, you probably won't be able to raise the funds needed for the Least Cost Concept.

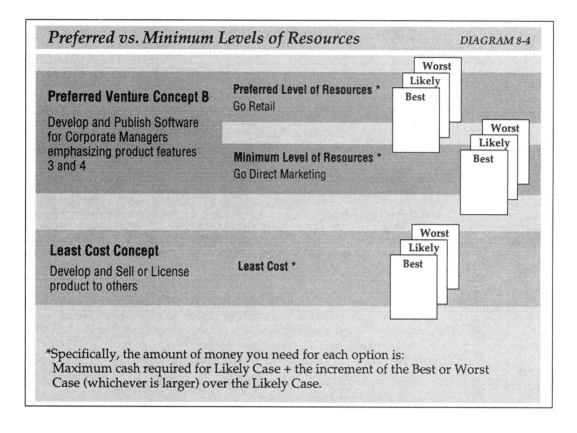

Preferred vs. Minimum Levels of Resources   *DIAGRAM 8-4*

Preferred Venture Concept B

Develop and Publish Software for Corporate Managers emphasizing product features 3 and 4

Preferred Level of Resources *
Go Retail

Minimum Level of Resources *
Go Direct Marketing

Least Cost Concept

Develop and Sell or License product to others

Least Cost *

*Specifically, the amount of money you need for each option is:
Maximum cash required for Likely Case + the increment of the Best or Worst Case (whichever is larger) over the Likely Case.

Let me restate what was said in Chapter Two: neither the Minimum Level Of Resources nor the Least Cost Concept assume an undercapitalized position. Both represent an appropriate capitalization, a threshold capitalization, for the particular way you are pursuing your customer opportunity. You cannot always compare them to the range of alternatives you must consider for your Preferred Level Of Resource because they are most likely apples and oranges. They can sometimes represent fundamentally different ways of pursuing the same opportunity.

Of course, the gap between the Preferred Level Of Resources and Minimum Level Of Resources is often much greater for larger and/or higher growth ventures. For instance, the gap for our venture was approximately $2 million($3 million for the Preferred Resource Option, while the Minimum Resource Option was about $1 million). Graphically, the two different options are shown in Diagram 8-5.

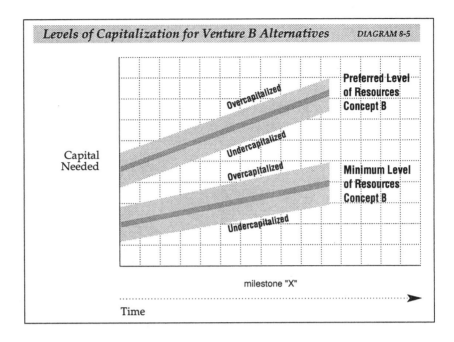

Levels of Capitalization for Venture B Alternatives　　*DIAGRAM 8-5*

Capital Needed

Overcapitalized

Undercapitalized

Overcapitalized

Undercapitalized

Preferred Level of Resources Concept B

Minimum Level of Resources Concept B

milestone "X"

Time

Overall, what you need to do is simplify a potentially confusing process so the number of venture concepts, and financial scenarios you consider are limited, eventually, to a few manageable variations. Diagram 8-6 outlines an overall procedure.

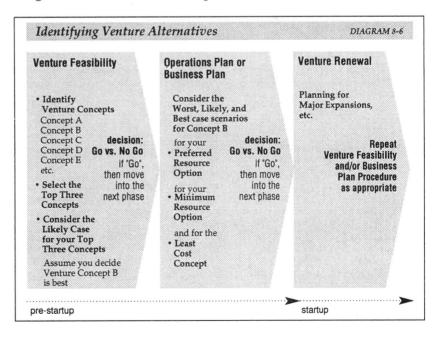

Identifying Venture Alternatives　　*DIAGRAM 8-6*

Venture Feasibility

• Identify
Venture Concepts
Concept A
Concept B
Concept C
Concept D
Concept E
etc.

decision:
Go vs. No Go
if "Go",
then move
into the
next phase

• Select the
Top Three
Concepts

• Consider the
Likely Case
for your Top
Three Concepts

Assume you decide
Venture Concept B
is best

Operations Plan or Business Plan

Consider the
Worst, Likely, and
Best case scenarios
for Concept B

for your
• Preferred
Resource
Option

decision:
Go vs. No Go
if "Go",
then move
into the
next phase

for your
• Minimum
Resource
Option

and for the
• Least
Cost
Concept

Venture Renewal

Planning for
Major Expansions,
etc.

Repeat
Venture Feasibility
and/or Business
Plan Procedure
as appropriate

pre-startup　　　　　　　　　　　　　startup

In the past, many successful entrepreneurs, managers, and business educators have realized that asking the right questions is often more difficult than providing a solution. Answering the questions once they are identified, is often the easier task.

The same is particularly true of identifying venture options or scenarios. Discovering the realistic options or identifying all the viable alternatives is generally harder, more creative, and more important than the task of coming up with viable solutions. However, a quandary has existed regarding the financial evaluation of alternatives once they were identified. If you identified too many you'd never be able to evaluate all of them and, if you did, you'd find yourself being inflicted by analysis paralysis.

Ronstadt's FINANCIALS allows you to perform your financial analysis so quickly that it opens the way for you to identify and weigh more options to really see which one is superior. At the very least, the program enables you to consider the Worst, Likely, and Best Case Scenarios for your Preferred Level Of Resources (i.e., the best way you think the venture should be implemented, your Minimum Level Of Resources for your Preferred Concept and the Least Cost Concept (i.e.,the option that allows you to get into business.) Too many entrepreneurs fail to develop the financial requirements for these fall-back venture options simply because:

a)   they are unaware of them or their importance;

b)   they suffer analysis fatigue just trying to develop the financial scenarios for their preferred way of starting their venture.

Summary: Some Practical Financing Advice

You need to use the Venture Feasibility Phase to think creatively about your proposed new venture or venture expansion. You must think particularly hard about the alternative ways to put your venture together and make it happen. Think about the venture concepts that satisfy a perceived customer need. Start by thinking about different customer/product groupings. What's most compelling about the needs of specific customer groups? What product features satisfy these compelling needs? Then proceed to ask what kind of business you can be and how you can produce and deliver your product to your customers.

Use your Business Plan or Operating Plan to develop the financial strategies and projections for a Preferred Level Of Resources and Minimum Level Of Resources. From personal experience, I can tell you it is reassuring to know that you have covered your financing needs for your Minimum Resource option or at least know where you can get these funds, as you negotiate the funds for your Preferred Level Of Resources. Raising money for your venture is often a stressful experience, especially as you approach startup. For more ambitious ventures, the stress is particularly acute as you incur the inevitable expenses needed to launch your venture. Burn rates increase dramatically (i.e., the weekly or monthly rate you "burn" cash to ignite your venture as you approach your launch date.) People must be hired. Facilities must be rented. Phone systems need to be installed. More furniture is needed. Timing becomes more incredibly sensitive. A one month delay in launch can mean thousands of extra dollars are needed to sustain the higher level of expenditures.

Considerable anxiety can be avoided if you not only consider a Minimum Level Of Resources, but also seek to finance it on a conditional basis. You may have to give someone a premium, but it will be well worth it should your financing fail to materialize for your Preferred Level Of Resources. You also won't have your back against the wall when negotiating the funds for your Preferred Level Of Resources.

Finally, you need to know your Least Cost Concept and its funding requirements in case you cannot raise *any* funds for your Preferred Concept. After all, the Least Cost Concept may be the only way to get into business (which, as we will see in Chapter Eleven, can be very important). But it may also be the only way for you to salvage what can become a considerable investment in your Preferred Concept which you've incurred during the Prestartup period, especially for High Growth Ventures.

Endnotes

1   New venture opportunities usually aren't found via brainstorming.
    See Karl Vesper's article, "New Venture Ideas: Do Not Overlook the
    Experience Factor," *Harvard Business Review*, July/August, 1979, pp.
    164-67. However, once an opportunity is found, creative brainstorm-
    ing is useful to look at different ways to make the venture happen.
    Furthermore, research on creativity has shown that

    a)   a positive relationship exists between the quantity of ideas and the
         quality of ideas ... specifically the better ideas are often among
         the last ones identified.

    b)   creativity can be learned and applied.

    Some good books on the subject are:

    - Robert von Oech, *A Whack On The Side Of The Head: How to
      Unlock Your Mind For Innovation*, Warner Books, New York, 1983.
    - Arthur B. Van Gundz, *Techniques Of Structured Problem Solving*,
      Van Nostrand Reinhold Company, New York, 1981.
    - Alex F. Osborn, *Applied Imagination*, 3rd edition, Charles
      Scribner's Sons, New York, 1979.

2   The distinctions between an Operations Plan and a Business Plan are
    based on the primary uses of the documents. When all is said and
    done, a Business Plan is primarily (though not exclusively) a "selling
    document" that is used to raise investment funds. Much of the infor-
    mation contained in it is expressly there to inform investors and/or
    bankers about your venture. However, many people start or expand
    ventures without any need for external investment funds. These in-
    dividuals are better off developing an Operations Plan. Besides
    being a less formal document, there is no need "to sell" the founder
    or entrepreneurial team, provide certain kinds of financial informa-
    tion, nor document a host of facts that you and other team members
    already know.

How Much Is My Venture Worth?

9

9

How Much?

At some point, every owner needs to estimate the current and future value of his or her venture. Even owners who have no need for funding should estimate the value of their venture. If nothing else, the answer lets them know if the venture they are planning or pursuing is worth what they think it is worth. It also tells them whether this value justifies the time and investment they've made plus what they anticipate making in the future.

But there is yet another reason. *The value a venture is likely to have in the future affects the value we place on the venture today.* For instance, a venture with potential sales of $100 million in five years is usually worth much more today than another venture whose fifth year sales are projected at only $10 million. Both ventures have some stated present value based on the value of their assets, their existing earnings and cash flow, and their future earnings and cash flow. Figuring out how much value is the purpose of venture valuation. It answers a central question of Entrepreneurial Finance: *How much is my venture worth?*

Venture Valuation Analysis

Much of our concern has focused on how much money your venture needs to get started or expand in some direction. But what value does this money have for your venture? This question is the same as asking: how much of your venture should you give up to get the money the venture needs? When the money is debt, you give up some of your venture's cash flow and profits in the form of interest payments. When the money is equity, you give up ownership shares that also have an impact on future cash flows:

- when dividends are declared
- when the ownership shares are sold, and/or
- when the venture's assets are sold.

How much interest you should pay on debt is an important question but one that does not immediately determine the value of your venture. For the purposes of our discussion, I will assume that you must sell equity to receive the money needed to create and/or expand your venture. Debt is often not an option or a prudent alternative for entrepreneurs during the Prestartup and Startup periods. Where debt is both prudent (in terms of risk) and possible, others have shown it is nearly always less expensive than equity. 1 Our chief concern, consequently, is the determination of equity value. What precisely should you pay (in equity) for a $100,000 investment? for a $500,000 investment? etc. How much equity should you give to a key member of your entrepreneurial team? How much "sweat equity" should the venture's founders receive for their efforts? These questions, and others, are determined only by ascribing some value to your venture.

Rules of Thumb

An investor once told me: "I need a 20% share of a company for any investment I make. It's just not worth getting involved for less." Another investor claimed he required at least 5 times his money. Such arbitrary rules are bad for both the investor and the company. They don't provide a "fairness basis" that is vital because both investor and entrepreneur must live together after the investment is made without feeling that one or the other got a better deal. It needs to be a "win-win" situation. In fact, if someone says they want to earn 20% for their investment, it can be shown mathematically (don't worry, we won't do it) that this statement is the same as saying they want to earn 3 times their investment over a six year period. Diagram 9-1 summarizes the relationship between rates of return, cash returns, and the investment's time period. 2

The table shown in Diagram 9-1 is particularly important because it shows the link between *targeted rates of return* (e.g., "I want to earn 50% on this investment"), cash multiples ("I want to earn eight times my cash investment"), and time (the investment must be realized within five years). The relationships in Diagram 9-1 also represent a fundamentally different way (i.e., a future way) to value equity compared to the present-based method of dividing shares based on equity contributions.

For example, suppose you have developed your venture idea through the feasibility phase. You've invested all your savings ($20,000) and your cash flow statement says your Preferred Resource Option — the way you'd like to start your venture — requires an additional investment of $118,000. Under the share of equity basis, the division of equity in your venture is:

	Investment	% Ownership Share
You:	$ 20,000	14.5%
Investor:	$118,000	85.5%
Total:	$138,000	100%

This division may strike you as grossly unfair but many deals are put together this way, especially after providing anywhere from 2% to 10% for "sweat equity." Assuming you received the high end for your idea, effort to date, foregone income, etc., your share is:

Cash Return	Investment Period						
	2 Years	**3 Years**	**4 Years**	**5 Years**	**6 Years**	**7 Years**	**8 Years**
2X	41.4%	26.0%	18.9%	14.9%	12.2%	10.4%	9.1%
3X	73.2%	44.2%	31.6%	24.6%	20.1%	17.0%	14.7%
4X	100.0%	58.7%	41.4%	32.0%	26.0%	21.9%	18.9%
5X	123.6%	71.0%	49.5%	38.0%	30.8%	25.8%	22.3%
6X	144.9%	81.7%	56.5%	43.1%	34.8%	29.2%	25.1%
7X	164.6%	91.3%	62.7%	47.6%	38.3%	32.0%	27.5%
8X	182.8%	100.0%	68.2%	51.6%	41.4%	34.6%	29.7%
9X	200.0%	108.0%	73.2%	55.2%	44.2%	36.9%	31.6%
10X	216.2%	115.4%	77.8%	58.5%	46.8%	38.9%	33.4%
11X	231.7%	122.4%	82.1%	61.5%	49.1%	40.9%	35.0%
12X	246.4%	128.9%	86.1%	64.4%	51.3%	42.6%	36.4%

Cash Returns, Investment Periods & Rates of Return   DIAGRAM 9-1

	Investment	% Ownership Share
You:	$ 20,000 plus 10% "sweat equity"	24.5%a
Investor:	$118,000	75.5%
Total:	$138,000	100%

a) 14.5% + 10%

Still unfair, you cry — and perhaps so, but the only way to alter this venture valuation in a significant way is to consider the division of equity under a different frame of reference ... one that looks to the future value of your enterprise.

For instance, the same person making the investment of $118,000 may be very happy earning three times this investment when you sell your store in five years. Diagram 9-1 shows this return of $354,000 (3 * $118,000) represents nearly 25% return on investment. Five years hence, your first year sales of $330,000 will have grown to roughly $500,000 (at 11% growth per year). The ownership shares that result are shown below for a range of venture values that are based on a simple multiple of sales (ranging from 1 to 2 times sales).

	1X	1.5X	2X
Venture Value:	$500,000	$750,000	$1,000,000
Investors Share: At 3 Times Investment or $118,000	$354,000	$354,000	$ 354,000
Balance To Owner:	$146,000	$396,000	$ 646,000
% Venture Value:	100%	100%	100%
% Investor's Share:	71%	47%	35%
% Owner's Share:	29%	53%	65%

(**X** = *Last Year of Sales or $500,00 In This Case*)

At all three levels of venture valuation your owner's share is higher than the share you receive under a division of equity that reflects the percentage of equity contributed, even after sweat equity is added to the calculation. Using a future targeted return to determine equity division means your investor will receive at least a 25% return while you retain the upside potential. For instance, your 65% share (if the venture is sold at two times sales) results in very different returns to you as the owner, specifically $401,000, as shown below:

	Share of Equity	**Targeted Return**
	100%	100%
Owner's Share with 10% Sweat Equity:	24.5%	65%
Dollar Value	$245,000	$646,000
Difference:	$401,000	

"Simple" Valuation

A better approach to determining the present value of a venture is to ask first — not what kind of future return you or an investor desires, but —What is the likely future value of the venture at some appropriate point in time? A shortcut method I call "simple valuation" is often used to project future value. This "simple valuation" means that:

$100,000 for 10% of a venture indicates that the venture is worth $1,000,000 now. In other words, if 10% is worth $100,000, the remaining 90% must be worth $900,000 for a total of $1,000,000.

||||||||||||||||| **NOTE** *$100,000/.10 = $1,000,000. This formula is useful when the amounts and percentages aren't so obvious, e.g., the valuation of a $323,000 investment for 16% ($323,000/.16) equals $2,018,750.*

Of course, your venture is not really worth $1,000,000 now (at 10% for $100,000) if you had to liquidate it. The $1,000,000 reflects a present value based on future potential or future value. The question then becomes: Is this valuation in line with what other firms have received at similar point in time in their venture evolution? Such comparisons are often difficult. They may be okay for gross valuations to test if something is way out of line, but they are only relevant if the ventures being compared are looking at the same stream of future cash flows and earnings.

To reach a more sensible and accurate answer, you need to project these earnings out into the future and then place some present value on them. In other words, here's the value of your venture today *given* what it is likely to achieve in the "foreseeable" future in terms of cash flows, earnings, and, any number of other criteria.

The word "foreseeable" is very important, in my view. There are, for instance, valuation methods that consider multiple points in time over long periods — seven, ten, or more years. I think someone would have to make a compelling case (e.g., special astrological gifts) to convince me that the foreseeable future is anything over five years. Let's face it, making approximations for years two through five is precarious enough for most ventures.

Two Suggested Methods of Valuation

Two related methods of venture valuation are useful to know. Both methods relate value to the future sales and earnings of your venture.

The first method is called the *Conventional Venture Capital Method of Valuation*. The second method is an extension of the *Conventional Method*, and is known as the *First Chicago Method*.

The Conventional Method of Venture Valuation

The *Conventional Method* derives the value of your venture by:

a) estimating the level of sales revenue you will realize after x years (let's say five years), and the rate of sales growth you will realize during those years.

b) Multiplying your fifth year revenues by your expected after-tax profit margin to arrive at fifth year earnings after tax.

c) multiplying your fifth year earnings after tax by some accepted "price-earnings ratio." (The price earnings ratio is a multiple that represents how many times earnings per share can be divided into the actual market price of stock of comparable companies that are publicly traded on a stock exchange. For instance, if the stock is selling for $15 per share and the earnings per share is equal to $1.00, then the price earnings ratio (or P/E) equals 15.)

d) The future value of the company is then multiplied by a *discount or present value factor* that represents a minimum rate of return over the five years. These discount factors represent the present value of one dollar that will be received at some point in the future given a targeted rate of return. Diagram 9-2 presents a table of discount factors for investment time periods lasting up to nine years and targeted returns ranging from 25% to 60%. For instance, this table says that the value of a dollar *now* is a little over eighteen cents (.186) if I must wait five years to receive it and if I want a 40% return on my money.

Consequently, the *future value* of a venture that will experience yearly sales growth of 50%, growing from $3 million to $22.8 million in five years, with a profit after tax margin of 10%, and a price earnings ratio of 12 at that time, is $27.4 million. The *present value* of the $27.4 million at 40% annual return is (27.4 * .186) = $5.1 million (where .186 is the discount factor).

If the money you are seeking is $1,000,000, then its value in equity equals:

$$\frac{\$1,000,000}{5,100,000} = 19.7\%$$

Based on your projections, the Conventional Method of valuation says you should expect to sell 19.7% or approximately 20% of your equity to obtain the $1,000,000 you need for your venture.

The First Chicago Method of Venture Valuation

The great value of the *First Chicago Method* is that it sets up a way for us to determine how much equity to pay for an investment while considering multiple scenarios — not just one scenario. These scenarios can be a Worst, Likely, Best Case, or they can represent even more extreme outcomes, such as Bare Bones Survival, or Liquidation.

The steps are:

1   Calculate the present value of each scenario using the Conventional Valuation Method.

2   Assess the fractional probability that each scenario will occur. The total of the probabilities here must equal 1.00.

3   Multiply the present value of each scenario by its probability factor.

4   Add up the "adjusted present values" for all scenarios.

5   Divide the amount of money being sought by the venture's adjusted present value.

Discount Factors   DIAGRAM 9-2

Present Value of One Dollar Earned at a Future Point in Time

Investment Period	25%	30%	35%	40%	45%	50%	55%	60%
2yrs	.641	.592	.549	.510	.476	.444	.417	.391
3yrs	.513	.455	.407	.364	.328	.296	.269	.244
4yrs	.410	.350	.301	.260	.226	.197	.173	.153
5yrs	.328	.270	.223	.186	.156	.132	.112	.095
6yrs	.262	.207	.165	.133	.108	.088	.072	.093
7yrs	.210	.159	.122	.095	.072	.059	.047	.037
8yrs	.168	.123	.091	.068	.051	.039	.030	.023
9yrs	.134	.094	.067	.048	.035	.026	.019	.015

The example, shown in Diagram 9-3, combines the Conventional and First Chicago Methods, and assumes different growth rates, profitability rates, and price earning ratios for the three different scenarios.

Row #1 shows base year revenues of three million dollars for each scenario.

Three different growth rates are shown in Row #2. The rate of 50% for Moderate Success may seem high, but remember, these are the first years of a startup where successful launches may experience growth rates between 100% and 200% as sales double and sometimes triple.

Revenue
The Revenue in Row #3 is the compounded product of multiplying the base year by the annual growth rate.

Profit After Tax
The Profit After Tax in Row #5 is the product of Row #3 multiplied by the decimal equivalent of Row #4.

Future Value of the Venture
The Future Value of the Venture is calculated by multiplying Profit After Tax (Row #5) times an estimated Price Earnings Ratio (Row #6).

Present Value of the Venture
The Present Value of the Venture is calculated by multiplying the venture's Future Value (Row #7) by a Present Value Factor (.186) taken from Diagram 9-2 that assumes a need for a 40% return earned on an investment held for five years.

Adjusted Present Value
The Adjusted Present Value is calculated by multiplying the Present Value of each scenario by the estimated probability that each scenario will happen.

Finally, these adjusted values are added together and divided into the investment needed. The quotient (38.8%) represents the amount of equity ownership you need to give up for the $1,000,000.

Example Of First Chicago Method Of Valuation   Diagram 9-3

	Moderate Success	Bare Bones Survival	Liquidation in 3rd Year
1. Base Year Revenues	$ 3 mil.	$ 3 mil.	$ 3 mil.
2. Growth Rate	50%	10%	0%
3. Revenue 5th Year	$22.8 mil.	$4.4 mil.	$3 mil.
4. % Profit After Tax	10%	2%	0%
5. Profit After Tax	$2.28 mil.	$ 90,000	$ 0
6. Price Earnings Rati	12	5	N/A
7. Future Value of Venture	$27.4 mil.	$450,000a	$200,000b
8. Present Value Factor for Discount Rate Assuming 40% Over Five Years	.186	.186	.186
9. Present Value of Each Venture Scenario	$5.1 mil.	$ 83,700	$ 37,200
10. Probability That Each Scenario Will Happen (Total = 1.00)	.5	.3	.2
11. Adjusted Present Value	$2,550,000	$ 22,320	$ 7,440

12. Combined Adjusted Present Value of Venture	$2,582,550
	(2,550,000 + 25,110 + 7,440)

13. Investment	$1,000,000

14. Required Ownership Given Investment	$\dfrac{\$1,000,000}{\$2,582,550} = 38.8\ \%$

a) Assumes an acquisition.
b) Assumes net liquidation value after three years.

Multiple Financings and Dilution

A basic assumption of this book is that multiple financings are frequent occurrences and, in many situations, should be sought by entrepreneurs rather than avoided. However, when multiple *equity* financings occur, you need to know how dilution works since investors may often ask for anti-dilution rights.

Webster defines "dilute" as: "1.) to thin down or weaken by mixing with water or other liquid." It's an apropos description of what happens when you sell additional equity. The new equity reduces or "thins down" your equity position along with other existing investors. Furthermore, if one or more of these existing investors has anti-dilution rights, then you get "thinned down" even more as you absorb the dilution they have avoided. Here's how dilution works over three rounds of financing. (See Diagram 9-4) The assumptions are: smaller amounts of equity are raised for Rounds 1 and 2 to move into the startup period. Round 3 requires substantial funds to launch the venture.

|||||||||||||| NOTE *The key calculation is the multiplication of each investor's initial equity portion by the amount of equity being raised, e.g., for Round 2, the owner's 90% equity position is multiplied by 20%.*

(.90 * .20 = .18)
Then   90% - 18% = 72%

Dilution Effects			Diagram 9-4
Investors	Initial Equity	Dilution	Ending Equity
Owner	100%	0	100%
Round 1: Amount Of Equity Sold is 10%			
Owner	100%	10%	90%
Partner	—	—	10%
Round 2: Amount Of Equity Sold is 20%			
Owner	90%	18%	72%
Partner	10%	2%	8%
Investors A	—	—	20%
Totals	100%	20%	100%
Round 3: Amount Of Equity Sold is 40%			
Owner	72%	28.8%	43.2%
Partner	8%	3.2%	4.8%
Investor A	20%	8.0%	12.0%
Investor B	—	—	40.0%
Totals	100%	40%	100%

Notice how Investors A and B have majority ownership (52%) at the end of Round 3. Also, if Investors A had non-dilution rights then the ending equity positioning would be calculated as if you and your partner had 100% of the initial equity (i.e. 90% and 10% respectively from Round 2), but the dilution would still be subtracted from your Round 3 initial equity positioning. For example:

Assume Investors "A" Have Zero Dilution			
Owner	72%	36% a	36%
Partner	8%	4% b	4%
Investor A	20%	0	20%
Investor B	—	—	40%
Totals	100%	40%	100%

a) .90 * .40 = .36
b) .10 * .40 = .04

Investors A and B now own 60% of the venture. The moral of this latter example is that entrepreneurs should avoid anti-dilution requests like the plague. Only under special circumstances should they be granted. 3

Finally, let me say that investors and entrepreneurs should not be afraid of dilution *per se*. The notion of a smaller percentage of a much greater pie is a valid one. Presumably the equity being sold will produce a disproportionately larger pie or the investment will not be made in the first place. Getting "diluted down" is not necessarily a bad thing — as long as all are diluted equally.

Getting to the End Game

The principal tool for valuing the price of equity funds remains venture valuation. It is not a precise tool, but you can calculate some approximate numbers for the amount of equity you should give up under certain circumstances. Even under the simplest and most arbitrary of valuations, these assumptions are, in fact, being made. Often you can save yourself significant chunks of equity by being explicit about these assumptions. Conversely, you may not walk away from a good deal that you thought was bad because your intuitive valuation of your venture was unrealistically located in the upper stratosphere.

Also, you can supplement your valuations with other information. In one sense, valuation is the end game of Entrepreneurial Finance. But to play a good end game, you need to play a good opening, i.e., develop meaningful financial projections. You also need to play a good middle game, i.e., analyze these projections along several lines. Here you need to understand more than cash flow to understand the financial health of your venture. As we saw in Chapter Six, a working knowledge of several other tools is also needed to assess the current and future well-being of your enterprise. Contribution and breakeven analysis provide insight about the potential risks of producing certain products and services versus others. Various ratios and profitability measures monitor the pulse and temperature of your venture. *Together, these "health tools" indicate not only the risk position and the kind of funds your venture requires, they also help you to place a value on the use of this money.*

For instance, you can justify a higher amount than comparable ventures if *percentage analysis* of your projections reveals that your venture can justifiably earn higher gross margins and net profit margins compared to other similar ventures. Similarly, higher profitability over time means higher valuations. Liquidity also has a valuation impact. In terms of projections (and past results for existing ventures), you want to see a scenario that shows greater working capital positions each year. If this year's working capital is less than last year's, how can we grow faster this year than last year without borrowing or selling stock? Of course you may not always wish to grow faster. *But investors and others will value your company higher if they see growth potential and the "current" ability to finance this greater growth in the form of an increasing working capital position. Healthy Current and Acid Test Ratios will similarly result in higher valuations.* Likewise, greater asset productivity, faster turnover, and greater efficiency of assets means higher valuations compared to other ventures. *Ventures with products that are high contributors generally receive higher valuations ... especially when combined with lower sales breakevens as a percentage of projected sales.*

All these indicators have an impact on the value of a venture. But, as we shall now see, they have value *to you only if you know how to communicate their significance to the right people, at the right time.*

Endnotes

1   See Kenneth J. Hattan, "Financial Accounting And Strategy: A Very
    Brief Overview," Boston University, 1987, where he states the follow-
    ing: "People borrow money rather than raise equity because debt is
    cheaper than equity — in part, because the government acts as a
    partner in allowing companies to treat interest payments as a tax de-
    ductible expense. Hence, when we consider the cost of capital, we
    know that equity is the highest cost form of capital and debt costs
    less."

2   For those who wish to get into the finer points of valuation, I recom-
    mend the *QED Report On Venture Captital Formation*, QED Research,
    Inc., Palo Alto, California, 1987.

3   An example of a special circumstance is when two separate invest-
    ments are made in a venture but the second unexpectedly and quick-
    ly follows the first investment … let's say a month apart. In this in-
    stance you may want to treat both investments as one rather than
    dilute the first investors.

Where and How to Get the Money Your Venture Needs

10

10

Where and How?

A few years ago, I surveyed two large MBA classes of entrepreneur-ship students and asked them *where* they expected to raise the money they needed to start their ventures. The data indicated that the vast majority expected some or all of the funds would come from personal savings. (See Diagram 10-1). To a lesser extent, they thought the cash they needed to start a venture would also come from family, friends, partners, banks, or other individual investors. Hardly anyone felt they would raise money from other sources, specifically private placements, public offerings, Small Business Investment Corporations (SBICs), or professional venture capitalists.

Sources of Financing Expected to Use		Diagram 10-1
	% Day	% Evening
Personal Savings	94	87
Family	82	33 [1]
Banks	65	44
Partners	41	36
Other Individual Investors	29	26
Friends	12	15
SBICs	6	8
Venture Capitalists	0	3
Private Placement	0	0
Public Offering	0	0
Other	6	6

The lack of financing from the last source, venture capitalists, may surprise you. But this response is consistent with the facts — very few people are ever funded by venture capitalists, especially those starting new ventures. By "venture capitalists" I mean money obtained from one of approximately 800 companies whose stated purpose is to finance new and emerging ventures. In 1986 these companies financed about 1,300 companies, of which only slightly more than 200 were new ventures. The rest were refinancings of existing ventures, including leverage buyouts of many older, established businesses. 2

Now let me say that the Venture Capital industry is vital to our economy and that many VC-backed companies make noteworthy contributions to society. However, please do not forget that 200 plus investments represents no more than a smidgen of the 1.3 million ventures that were started last year. In other words, only one venture out of every 6,500 ventures started last year received Venture Capital money.

I raise these points in order to place the question of *where* you will likely raise money into proper perspective. There are, no doubt, some major differences that exist between my former MBA students and those who actually start ventures; however, I do not believe sources of financing is one of them. For all practical purposes, your sources of financing, after your own savings, are likely to be your Uncle Albert, the local loan officer of your bank, other private individuals and/or supplier financing. The difficulty is that each of these probable sources has different interests when it comes to investing in you and your venture.

Communicating Your Venture's Financial Needs to Different Groups

Taking control of your financial destiny means comprehending and communicating the significance of those critical numbers that define your venture's present position and future direction. You must identify and comprehend the key numbers *yourself* before you can communicate them to others.

Attaining full comprehension of these numbers means you need to internalize them. And to internalize your projections, you must simplify them. Detail is necessary to build your financial projections. A measure of detail gives you confidence in your numbers. But you cannot retain reams of detail, nor can you track every detail as your venture unfolds. Ken Olsen's experience as the founder and leader of Digital Equipment Corporation (DEC) bears remembering:

> *"We didn't have a big volume of spreadsheets and dozens of colored graphs. We did have simple profit and loss statements and simple balance sheets, and when American Research (a venture capital company) could see that these financial plans were in our head and in our heart, that we made them, understood them, remembered them, and they were simple enough to be a model for us to run the company daily and weekly and monthly using them as a model ... (then) they committed to invest in us without waiting for a final beautifully bound proposal."*
>
> *"Today, when plans are done by computer or by staff, they have more detail than one can keep in his head. I sometimes fear that the elegant mathematics of a P&L and balance sheet loses its usefulness when people put too much detail into it."* [3]

Simplification is a vital prerequisite for effective communication of your venture's needs to others. However, a concise presentation does not insure success if you present the wrong things or fail to emphasize what's most important. Let's consider what to communicate and how best to communicate your financial information to different groups. As you might expect, which numbers are important depends upon who is reviewing the financial projection: loan officers, informal investors, family investors, prospective team members, versus professional venture capitalists. Effective communication means you need to be selective. It is your job to determine which numbers they need to see. Moreover, they certainly should not get all the results you've mined, only what they need, and most want to see.

What Level of Detail?

Projections are not accounting statements. As we discussed in Chapter 4, you do not want to burden yourself or others by reporting, for instance, that Projected Net Sales are $2,195,283, when $2,195,000 or even $2.2 million is much easier to retain (and just as likely to occur).

Besides reducing the number of digits, you should also reduce the number of lines of information in your various financial statements — exclude those items that represent detailed breakdowns of major categories in terms of dollar amounts. For instance, the following seven-line Income Statement is much easier to absorb and retain than one with thirty or forty lines of detail.

Income Statement $ (000's)

Net Sales	$ 2.2
Cost Of Sales	.5
Gross Profit	1.7
Operating Expenses	1.0
Profit Before Taxes	.7
Taxes	.3
Net Income	$ .4

What to Communicate?

Numbers are only part of what you want to communicate, albeit an important part. While there are always exceptions to the rule, Diagram 10-2 shows what my experience suggests are the major areas to emphasize for different sources of financing.

Numbers for Friends and Family

Whether they ask or not, friends and relatives often want to know "what you've put into the venture" beyond your ideas and sweat. Other sources want to know this information, but friends and family may need to know little more. A simple projected Income Statement may be sufficient.

Often relatives and close friends do not expect part of your company or even a "real return" on this money. But they generally want to know when they can expect to get their money back.

Despite the "favorable terms," don't delude yourself into thinking that these funds are free. They can have an all too real cost that results in shattered relationships. Some guidelines:

- Be explicit about the risks; don't hide or understate them.
- Be explicit about the terms. Write them down and share this written note with investing family members, e.g., "my understanding is ..."

What to Emphasize to Different Sources of Financing   Diagram 10-2

	What General Messages: What Are They Most Looking For?	What Numbers Specifically To Emphasize
1. Friends/Family	Your risk Sales/Profitability	What you have or have not invested and why
	Will I get my money back?	When repaid? Income Statement
2. Bank Loan Officers	The increased value this loan will produce for your venture	The Core Statements, emphasizing the Cash Flow Statement
	The 4-C's • your credit • your character • your collateral • your capacity (to repay)	Debt/Equity Ratios Interest Coverage Ratio Other Key Measures
3. Informal Investors	Your mission and the financial & psychic rewards they will accrue	The Core Statements (Compressed and showing minimum detail)
	Their "informal" involvement in your venture. How "cash out?"	When sufficient profits will occur Dividend payments, consulting income, or other means of payment.
4. Professional Venture Capitalists	Ability to create a "High Growth Venture" that will return 30-50% on invested equity per year	The Core Statements and Key Budgets
	Justification of first year sales new line When and how harvest money	

While money from family and friends has its dangers, you should not arbitrarily rule it out. Many of our greatest corporations were started with family money. There's nothing to be ashamed about. Under the right circumstances, it's the best money you will ever find.

Numbers for Your Banker

What do lenders want to see? Lenders want to know:

- How much you want to borrow
- What you want the money for
- When you will be able to repay the loan
- When you will be able to pay the interest
- If your venture can survive a setback in its plans
- What security is available for the loan

Despite all the great things you have said about your venture and regardless of how convinced you are that your concept is the best thing to come down the pike since sliced bread, lenders will look at your venture with a focus on these very "typical" banker questions. Remember, it's their job to protect the assets of the bank.

Their chief interest is your venture's ability to repay the loan. Next, they are interested in your ability to repay if the venture cannot — they will want to see your personal financial statements. Their decision about your ability to repay is based on whether or not you qualify regarding the "4-C's" of lending — Credit, Character, Collateral, and Capacity.

In some instances, you may be asked to provide a loan proposal or you may decide to present one to your loan officer. You can usually use all or parts of your business plan.[4] At the very least, your business plan will enable you to quickly write the required proposal. Be certain to include the following:

1 *A Summary Page:* provide your name, address, the name of the company, and the amount of the loan. Also provide two brief paragraphs that state
   a   the purpose of the loan and
   b   how you can expect to repay it.

2 *A Business Fact Sheet:* provide a brief profile of the company, its purpose, age, legal organization, employees, and a summary of key financial facts — recent sales, margins, and any key assets or liabilities. If relevant, note any prior loans with the bank and the company's history with the bank.

3 *Proposal For Funds:* Describe in more detail why you need the funds, how they will be used, what value they will produce, and how you will repay them.

4   *Executive Profiles*: your experience, role, skills, and any other information that reinforces your professional standing and character.

5   *Financial Projection*: you must be clear about your assumptions.

6   *Past and Current Accounting Statements*: These may include your personal income tax statements as well as your company's statements.

Eight Rules for Borrowing From Your Banker [5]

1   *Select your bank carefully,* preferably one that knows you. Get a letter of introduction, preferably from your former banker if you're moving to a new region or community.

2   *Call and make an appointment.* Treat your banker like a professional. Don't just "drop in".

3   *Know what to bring.* Be certain you know what they want you to bring to the meeting or what they'll need to make a decision. Have them mail loan forms to you ahead of time, if possible.

4   *Be prepared. Spend four to eight hours getting ready.* One expert states that "fewer than 10% of prospective borrowers came to the bank adequately prepared." [6]

5   *Prepare and know your financial projections.* Don't depend on your accountant unless he or she will come to the bank with you. Even then, be certain you understand the key numbers and what they mean.

6   *Be ready to guarantee your venture loans personally.* Unless you've been in business for several years, don't expect the bank to loan you money without evidence that you are ready to put some of your personal assets on the line. Be certain you think about this commitment beforehand. Just how far can you go without jeopardizing the well being of you and your family?

7   *Don't hide things. Be trustful and candid, even if it hurts.* Chances are a good banker will discover what you're holding back anyway. You need to provide all the pertinent information so you can fully utilize your banker's expertise.

8   *Become a customer of the bank's other services.* A valued customer will often obtain better service and consideration.

IIIIIIIIIIIIIII NOTE   **A Final Tip**

Many people use their savings, specifically savings accrued in the equity of their home, to start a venture. If you plan on refinanicing your home to finance your startup, you may want to consider opening an account as soon as possible with a smaller savings institution, in addition to your regular bank. Specifically, you want access to at least one bank that doesn't sell its mortgages on the secondary market . Most full service banks sell their mortgages and, to do so, they must insure that their mortgages meet a number of tests, especially an income test. This latter requirement may be a catch-22 for some entrepreneurs who plan to leave their jobs to work full-time on starting their venture. Without a guaranteed income, they can't qualify for the loan even if they earmark a portion of their savings to service the loan. Banks that hold their own mortgages can often work around this problem.

Numbers For Informal Investors

Enlisting the financial support of one or more informal investors often represents your best opportunity to finance a startup, assuming your investment and/or the investment of friends and relatives is insufficient to pursue your Preferred or Minimum Resource options. Most banks are not in business to be investors prior to startup unless they see an ironclad way of being repaid, and many vendors will feel the same way. Also, most professional venture capitalists won't give you a second look, unless you are one of the rare High Growth ventures that catches their fancy.

So how do you contact these informal investors? Who are they? What will they want to know about your venture? The reason they are called "informal" investors is a tip-off... there are no formal ways to contact them, with one recent exception. 7 Informal investors are a diverse group, often composed of wealthy entrepreneurs and other professionals who provide seed and early stage funds to new ventures for a variety of reasons. If you don't know anyone who fits this description, you need to "get the word out" so that somehow you tap into the informal investor's network. I use the word "network" because research reveals the existence of social networks composed of informal investors. As one study revealed:

Informal investors generally learn of investment opportunities through friends and business associates. During the course of this research, it was not uncommon to discover that finding one informal investor led to contacts with several others. A network of friends and associates appears to link these individuals. [8]

Don't assume (in your projections) that access to this network will be free. The fastest and surest way to penetrate a network of informal investors is to offer a finder's fee.

The diversity among informal investors means you need to be cautious about accepting generalizations about them. My experience with them indicates they don't fit any particular profile or stereotype. Some will invest only small amounts of money ($25,000 to $50,000) in ventures that are close to their homes (within driving distance), where they can have active participation, and where the venture is in an industry they know. Others will invest extremely large blocks of funds ($1 to 2 million) especially with co-investors, in unfamiliar industries without any active participation.

Numbers for Venture Capitalist and Other Institutional Equity Investors

"There's this horrible disease going around right now," says Robert J. Crowley, vice-president of Massachusetts Technology Development Corp., a state-owned venture firm. "It's called spreadsheet-itis. It's the most common ailment in business plans today. And the venture capitalists blame word processors and spreadsheet software." 9

What then do they want to see if it isn't 48 pages of spreadsheets? The chief interests of venture capitalists are:

- **Market size, growth, and future valuation**
  Is the market large enough for you to become a $20 to $100 million dollar company in the next five to six years. Subsidiary issues are the existence of high operating leverage and your ability to achieve first year sales. While venture capitalists will want five years of projections, it's usually the first year they're most interested in. 10

- **Five years of P&Ls and Balance Sheets**
  These are usually divided as follows:
  Twelve months for the first year, four quarters for the second year, plus three years of annual data; or Eight quarters covering the first two years and annual data thereafter.

- **Key budgets given the nature of your venture**
  For instance, if your venture is R&D intensive, then a detailed R&D Budget is appropriate.

The key message on financials for venture capitalists is to keep it simple. Present a summary of your likely financial scenario. If they want to know more about your Best and Worst Case, they'll ask for it. You personally may need 48 pages of output for your Venture Financial Plan. But don't burden potential investors with this detail.

How to Present the Numbers Using Ronstadt's FINANCIALS

One of the subtle but powerful features of Ronstadt's FINANCIALS is its ability to be highly selective about what you communicate in printed or graphic form. This capability allows you to avoid "spreadsheet-itis."

First, you can simplify Supporting, Core, and Analytic Statements by hiding rows. What you see is what gets printed.

Second, you can print selected rows if you do not wish to print an entire statement. For example, you may want to show only Net Sales and Net Profits. Even though these rows are not contiguous (or located right next to each other) you can "mark" and print them together by selecting the print menu item that says "Print Marked Rows."

Third, you can consolidate monthly data into quarters or annual totals and then print the quarterly or yearly data interleaved with the monthly data by simply pressing two keys — or you can turn the monthly data off and just print the quarterly or annual totals. The latter is especially useful when printing the Breakeven and Key Measures Statements, since generally you only want to see the annual figures.

Fourth, you can similarly display percentages with a single keystroke and then print them for individual statements with another keystroke. The percentages will be calculated off the row your cursor is located on, e.g., if your cursor is on Net Sales the percentages will be taken as a per cent of Net Sales. Percentages are interleaved automatically between the absolute values for different time periods. However, you can turn off the absolute values and just view, print, or graph the percentages.

Fifth, you can create one or more additional statements that present rows copied from other statements. Perhaps you want to show a "Summary Statement" that includes one or two rows from the Revenue Statement, the Income Statement, the Balance Sheet, the Cash Flow, the Breakeven Statement, and/or the Key Measures Statement. Also, you may want to add one or two new measures you've defined that don't already exist. Just about whatever you have in mind, Ronstadt's FINANCIALS can print it.

You can also graph just about whatever you want without leaving the program. To graph Net Sales, you simply "mark" the row, and then go the Graph Menu, select the kind of graph you want (line, bar, stacked bar, or pie) and graph it. Graph labels can be edited if necessary. The graph is printed by simply selecting the "Print Graph" option and pressing the Return key.

You can graph up to ten rows; however, it usually doesn't make sense to graph more than two or three items. Remember, simplify your presentation. One way to do this is to cut down on the time periods being graphed. Often it makes sense to build your projections on a monthly basis but present them graphically on a quarterly basis. It's easier to read a bar chart or a stacked bar with four columns of information instead of twelve columns.

The great selectivity of Ronstadt's FINANCIALS regarding printing and graphing is enhanced by another feature that is unique to the program. Specifically, the ability to display multiple financial scenarios at the same time on the computer's screen means you can print and graph common rows across these financial scenarios. For example, you can print or graph the breakeven, gross profit margin, etc. for three or four different scenarios just by making a few intuitively obvious selections. Private investors, venture capitalists, and your banker are often interested in this comparative information, yet they rightfully do not want to wade through three or four sets of projections to get the information.

Summary: Moving through the Forest

Being able to tailor your information and presentation is an important criterion for success. You may never get the chance to pursue your venture if you don't first convince a relative, a banker, or an investor to provide the money you need to start or expand your venture. The first step in tailoring detailed financial information is to simplify it.

The simplification of your financial projections will enhance your comprehension of this information and your ability to communicate it to others. It will allow you to see and understand the key relationships that drive your venture. It is easy to get lost in a forest of financial details. The trees that obscure your view of the big picture are not just created from analysis but also from the details of day-to-day operations that have financial implications. As Ken Olsen accurately described earlier in this chapter, it is the elegance of a simple P&L and Balance Sheet that's crucial for success. That doesn't mean their construction isn't messy and detail-laden at first. But these numbers must eventually become simple if they are to serve as a strategic and operating map through a forest of bewildering detail ... a forest that obscures entrepreneurial success from our vision ... a forest where pathways leading to venture failure are hardly discernable from those leading to success.

It is the distinctions between these two pathways, one leading to entrepreneurial success, the other to entrepreneurial failure that must now capture our concern.

Endnotes

1   Evening students, being older, employed, and for the most part, financing their own educations, apparently expected less financial involvement from family members compared to younger day students.

2   By 1985, Venture Magazine's *Guide To International Venture Capital*, Simon and Schuster, New York, 1985, p. 26, listed 780 U.S. venture capital companies. For the same year, *Pratt's Guide To Venture Capital Sources*, Ninth Edition, Venture Economics, Wellesley, MA, 1985, p. 145, list over 700 companies in the United States and Canada. The consensus is that this number has grown since 1985. The number of deals by stage of financing is reported monthly by *Venture Magazine's* "The Venture Index of Venture Capital Activity." For instance, the November, 1987 edition states that approximately 1,360 deals were financed by venture capitalists, of which 227 were "seed and startup;" 94 were "latter stage;" 984 were "follow-on" deals; and 55 leverage buyouts.

3   Ken Olsen, *Unpublished Commencement Speech*, MIT, June 1, 1987

4   A fuller treatment is provided by Joan G. Ford, in "A Dozen Ways To Borrow Money, Finding Capital: Part 1," *Inc. Magazine,* Boston, MA. This article describes the twelve different kinds of loans plus how to put together a loan proposal.

5   I'm indebted to Michael Celello for his "Tips From A Banker," and for most of these rules, reprinted in *Inc. Magazine's* "Finding Capital: Part 1," Boston, MA

6   *Ibid.*

7   The exception is Venture Capital Network, Inc., P.O. Box 882, Durham, NH 03824, which charges a small fee to provide information about entrepreneurs and their ventures to participating private investors.

8   The groundbreaking work on informal investors has been done by
    William Wetzel. See his article "Informal Investor — When and
    Where To Look," in Arthur Lipper's *Guide To Investing In Private
    Companies*, Dow Jones-Irwin, Homewood, IL, 1984, pp. 168-176.

9   See "Big Plans: Business Plans Aren't Getting Better — They're Getting
    Longer," *Inc. Magazine*, February, 1987, p. 64.

10 To see what else venture capitalists are interested in (along with what
    they definitely aren't interested in), I highly recommend *Business
    Plans That Win $$$* by Stanley R. Rich and David E. Gumpert, Harper
    & Row, New York, 1985.

Entrepreneurial Success and Taking Control of Your Decision Making

11

11

Success and Control

Entrepreneurial success and failure are close cousins. Sometimes they are hard to tell apart from afar, but up close some clear distinctions are emerging that weren't visible too long ago.

Until the early 1980s, the people who were most knowledgeable about entrepreneurship uniformly described and analyzed entrepreneurs as though they were all cut from the same cookie mold. Instead of one species, we know today that "genus entrepreneuris" is composed of many species. For instance, in this book, we've classified their venture activities as Lifestyle, Smaller High-Profit, and High-Growth ventures. Other useful classifications exist that help us to better understand and help entrepreneurs.[1] Some no doubt remain undiscovered. But the point is that entrepreneurs are not one animal but many.

A basic reason for distinguishing between different kinds of entrepreneurs, perhaps the only legitimate reason, is to distinguish better between success and failure. As motivations, goals, and execution differs between entrepreneurs, what constitutes success or failure also differs. What represents a smashing success for a Lifestyle entrepreneur may be insignificant or outright failure for a High Growth entrepreneur.

Consequently, the ultimate objective is to distinguish between successful versus unsuccessful entrepreneurs for each species of entrepreneur. It's also the dichotomy we know the least about. What we do know is that defining success and failure is never easy nor clean. We also know that just identifying the "unsuccessful ones" is particularly difficult...one would think they are a rare species, if not an extinct one.

Yet we are told frequently in the press, textbooks, and other media that risks of failure are quite high. Terrorizing numbers are trotted out that you have, for example, a 50% chance of failing within five years. But then where are all the failures? Frankly, the numbers have been confused and misread by some and maintained as true by others who have a self interest in scaring you.

What then do we really know about entrepreneurial success and failure? We know that nearly all references to entrepreneurial success and failure focus on *venture success and failure,* rather than focusing on the longer-term success or failure of the entrepreneur(s). Unfortunately, the doomsday focus on venture failure is misleading and harmful. This harm was perhaps stated best by Albert Shapiro, a pioneer in the field of Entrepreneurial Studies, in a classic piece, "Numbers That Lie." [2]

> *One of the biggest barriers to entrepreneurship is the widespread no-tion that almost all new businesses fail in very short order. This myth discourages young people who might think of going into busi-ness for themselves, and it influences important people who affect startups, like bankers, government officials, and professors (who ought to know better). Why start a business when you know you're doomed to fail?*
>
> *The most popular belief is that 90% of all new companies fail in their first year. This is the number my students give me year after year, and I keep wondering where it got started and how it got such wide currency.*
>
> *My favorite "statistic," however, came from a newspaper column answering the questions of children; it was printed, ap-propriately enough, on the same page with the comics, and stated seriously that all businesses fail "eventually." I can go along with that.*

One thing is certain: if we wish to approximate the true odds of entrepreneurial success or failure, we need to distinguish clearly be-tween venture failure versus entrepreneurial career failure. *The con-cept of an entrepreneurial career must become ingrained in our thinking when we consider the ultimate success or failure of an entrepreneur ... for, as we shall see, another kind of entrepreneur — the multiple venture entrepreneur — survives in surprisingly large numbers.*

Who Fails?

Pretend for a moment that we have a magical microscope that iden-tifies large numbers of venture founders at random points in time whenever these entrepreneurs realized or approached *venture failure*. If we looked at enough of them, what we now know suggests we'd see:

- A large number of them who are *Near Venture Failures* yet who ultimately are successful.
- A lesser number of them who are *Temporary Venture Failures* yet who ultimately are successful.
- A very small number of them who are *Permanent Career Failures* and who ultimately are forced to work for someone else.

The largest and most visible group we'd see under our micro-scope is the *Near Venture Failures*. For those self assured and per-haps cocky entrepreneurs who've experienced a smashing venture success, this group should provide pause and, hopefully, a measure of humility. For it's not hard to find many successful entrepreneurs who barely survived a close brush with financial disaster during their venture startups or even a partial venture failure they were able to survive. Henry Ford was only a few days from closing the Ford Motor Company before the cash needed to pay the weekly payroll materialized. Others less famous tell of some crisis they overcame that narrowly avoided disaster during the pre-startup or startup phases of their ventures. The closest brush with venture failure I've heard was a new high tech company that was being driven into bankruptcy by its creditors. The bankruptcy announcement was to be made first to employees in the presence of a court appointed official on a Friday afternoon at 3:30 P.M. The founder, however, had other ideas. He started an argument with the court official that rapidly warmed up and before the latter realized it, the time was 5:00 P.M. and the employees had left for the weekend. The announcement was rescheduled for early Monday morning, but it was never made. The founder was able to raise additional financing over the weekend and satisfy his creditors.

The *Temporary Venture Failures* are much less numerous. They are defined as entrepreneurs who experience one or more venture failures but go on to create a successful venture. Venture failure, does not just mean bankruptcy. It also means a venture that is discontinued or left to a passive existence because it has not achieved the goals set by the founder(s).

Actually, very few ventures go through bankruptcy each year — less than half of 1% of all the businesses in existence in any given year. 3 This number doesn't increase much even after we add those temporary failures that are forced to close up shop managing to avoid bankruptcy, yet still owing something to creditors. The good news is that "forced discontinuances" are much lower than suggested by the terrorizing numbers that are usually bandied about. Even when voluntary discontinuances are included, the rate is probably somewhere around 3% — i.e., 3 out of a 100 firms. 4 This percentage is roughly equal to the 24% national "disappearance rate" over five years for a large sample of U.S. companies and a 15% disappearance rate for high growth ventures reported recently. 5 Both figures (annualized at about 5% and 3% respectively) plus the 3% I've cited still overstate real discontinuances because we know that some ventures that "disappear" or discontinue are not always really discontinued. Some ventures are continued under new legal names and/or new ownership that just makes tracing them difficult.

The bad news is that forced discontinuances are higher for younger ventures versus older ventures. The same is probably true for voluntary venture discontinuances. Once a venture reaches a certain age, it has either entered the Post Startup phase and stabilized by realizing positive operating cash flows, or else it remains in a precarious startup mode with needs for additional financing.

Nevertheless, the actual number of all these discontinuances, while not irrelevant, is still misleading. *The real drawback of all these numbers on "venture failure," be they "disappearance rates" or "discontinuance rates," be they younger or older ventures, is that they don't cap-*

ture the number of "follow-on ventures" that are started successfully by the same entrepreneur.

Nor do venture data give us any hint of the dynamic process that's driving many entrepreneurs, including our Temporary Failures. Some ventures deserve to be put to rest. But often the experience gained and new opportunities revealed from starting and operating a venture allow their entrepreneurs to start additional ventures that they could not have possibly started without first starting the prior "failed" venture. This process is experienced by many entrepreneurs, including "Temporary Failures," but it is not limited to them. Even entrepreneurs with vibrant enterprises see new venture opportunities and, more often than not, start a second, third, etc. venture. 6 I call this entrepreneurial phenomenon *"The Corridor Principle"* and it explains why entrepreneurs start successive ventures.

The Corridor Principle states that the act of starting a venture propels you down a corridor of knowledge whereby you gather information about an industry, suppliers, emerging markets, new contacts for financial and other resources, etc. As you move down this corridor, you see what you could never have seen before starting your venture ... you see intersecting corridors leading to new venture opportunities.

For those on the brink of venture failure, their ability to identify and take advantage of these new venture corridors determines whether their entrepreneurial career failure is temporary or permanent. (See Diagram 11-1)

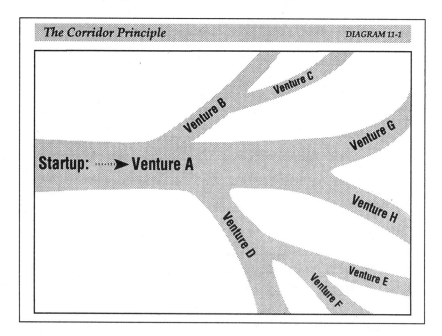

The Corridor Principle   DIAGRAM 11-1

The most severe casualties of entrepreneurship are the *Permanent Career Failures.* Unlike the Temporary Venture Failures, Permanent Career Failures do not start another venture. Instead, they do the one thing that makes most entrepreneurs sick just thinking about it. They go to work for someone else ... full-time employment with no particular end in sight prior to retirement. Let's be clear. I'm not talking about retired entrepreneurs who decide after 30 years of effective entrepreneuring to join the Peace Corps. Nor am I referring to Permanent Career *Exits* who've been quite successful as entrepreneurs, harvested a venture, and now find themselves working for a venture capital firm. What I mean by a Permanent Career Failure is someone who's been forced to discontinue one or more ventures after spending, in most cases, less than seven years as entrepreneur and often less than 3 years. 7

Many famous entrepreneurs experienced one or more venture failures. But somehow they were able to continue their entrepreneurial careers. Many more have experience with "Near Failure." Little is known about Permanent Career Failures who have prematurely ended their entrepreneurial careers and decided to work for someone else rather than start another venture. What is known suggests that:

- most Permanent Failures would still like to start another venture

- most Permanent Failures were driven from their careers as entrepreneurs for more than one reason but personal financial strain was a major reason in most instances. 8

Personal finance and venture finance are inextricably intertwined for entrepreneurs. Artificial separation of the two is necessary only for accounting purposes; otherwise the division is dangerous and misleading, as well as economically and emotionally irrational. How much personally should you risk financially on each venture? I think the answer depends greatly on your age, obligations, and the amount of wealth you have. For younger entrepreneurs with little or no real wealth, betting and losing "everything they have" is less likely to have catastrophic life consequences compared to a 40 year old couple who lose their life savings, their home, and the opportunity to put their two children through college.

I've known more than a few young entrepreneurs who've experienced a venture setback. Their response is usually to pick themselves up, dust off the financial and psychic debris, and start up again. If the setback has been particularly severe, the period of "recuperation" may last two or three years before they start another venture. However, the same quick healing is not true for older individuals and/or those who've amassed some significant savings or inherited substantial wealth. The responsibilities shift in these instances. These older individuals should not "bet the farm." If you have to invest all your assets, then the venture is too big for you now or in its present form. If you cannot scale it down, you must walk away unless "calculated risk-taking" degenerates into an unreasonable gamble, given your situation.

Often, a fruitful way out of this dilemma is to ask: Is there another smaller (and possibly different) venture I can start, which, if successful, I can use as a basis to start the "larger" venture (in terms of resource requirements) I'd like to, but shouldn't start now? This question is very similar to one you may have faced when buying a new home. Can I afford this place? What's the down payment (equity required)? What is the mortgage (debt), and what are the monthly cash outflows in principal, interest, etc.? Can I afford it? If not, can I afford the same kind of house (venture) that's unfinished or doesn't have all the extras? Or do I simply need to find a different house in a different neighborhood?

Why Do They Fail or Almost Fail?

The "surface" causes for Near and Temporary Venture Failure have been lumped together and are well documented. One expert cites six reasons which indicate that failure occurs because of the wrong: [9]

- choice of business
- education and experience
- kinds of collaborators
- location
- starting capital
- external forces.

Others conclude that many of these causes can be traced back to "poor or incompetent management" or the wrong kinds of personal skills and qualities.

From a cash flow perspective, the great majority of these ventures do not fail primarily from natural disasters (fire, flood, etc.); or from fraud or neglect (due to poor health, marital problems, etc.), but from lack of experience and/or incompetence. The financial expression of this experience/incompetence deficiency relates to an inability to design and implement a venture that has:

- sufficient dollar sales
- sufficient margins
- sufficient financial resources

All three financial reasons for venture failure are intertwined and reflect things like a weak knowledge of customers, an inappropriate or deficient product, weak execution, etc. All these reasons and others should be embodied in your projections. As such, all three reasons relate to "the numbers" and your ability to project accurate numbers that can be realized at a minimal level. Obviously, your financial projections cannot guarantee you sufficient sales, margins, and financial resources. But they can tell you what you need in resources to attain a projected level of sales with certain kinds of margins. And they let you compare projected results against actual results to see how well you are doing and whether minor adjustments or major action is needed.

What is the bare bones "minimal level" of accuracy for financial projections? The answer may surprise you. It relates to our discussion of types of failure. *The absolute minimal level of accuracy is the level that does not necessarily guarantee venture survival; rather it's the level of accuracy that guarantees financial survival that's sufficient to start another venture. As bad as venture failure can be, the real curse of entrepreneurship is NOT Temporary Venture Failure, but Permanent Career Failure.*

Some ventures should fail and some entrepreneurs should leave entrepreneuring. But, let's face it, the entrepreneurs who've failed at one venture have received an incredible education. We don't want them to be forced to leave. They should choose to leave because they clearly feel they can be more productive elsewhere. Some errors may occur here, but the ultimate misallocation of resources is to force a potentially successful entrepreneur into a non-entrepreneurial career. What if Ray Kroc, Berry Gordy, Steven Jobs, Thomas Watson, or Mary Kay Ash had failed and been forced to work for someone else for the rest of their lives. I have no doubt this kind of disastrous misallocation of human potential has already happened.

In this respect, the Corridor Principle has pervasive implications for entrepreneurs, especially potential entrepreneurs. *It says the primary goal for a first venture is not necessarily to start your "dream venture," or even earn above average financial returns, but to get into business.* This particular advice has merit for several reasons.

1   Most Permanent Failures start their first venture later (mid 30s to early 40s).

2   Entrepreneurial experience (i.e., the experience of going through the pre-startup and startup phases) is invaluable when creating a second, third, or follow-on venture. It also is invaluable when "creating a new venture within an existing venture," or otherwise taking an existing venture in a new direction.

3   Ownership skills and attitudes need to be developed and, I suspect, they are easier to develop when one is relatively younger and uninfected with an employee mentality that unconsciously conditions one's thinking after spending years, perhaps decades, working for someone else.

Ownership Skills and Entrepreneurial Success

Years ago, John Hendrick wrote a classic description about how he had to overcome the handicap of a college education in order to start his own business. He argued convincingly that although a college education is valuable and to be desired, it nevertheless can bias one from becoming an owner.

In the same vein, the Hendrick's article also supports the notion that new entrepreneurs often must "overcome the handicap of an employee mentality" when they start a business. 10 Most people do not automatically know how to be owners. Venture ownership skills and attitudes are not imprinted on our genes. They are skills and attitudes that need to be developed, honed, and refined. Entrepreneurial finance, i.e., the skill of financial strategy formulation and implementation for new ventures, is one of several critical ownership skills. My purpose is not to discuss these ownership skills now, but to indicate their importance for entrepreneurial success over the long haul, covering not necessarily one, but many ventures.

On Entrepreneurial Career Success

At the minimum, the road that leads to entrepreneurial success means handling venture success and/or venture failure in a productive way. It means staying sufficiently healthy, emotionally and financially speaking, so you can keep playing. Like an athlete, you may lose a game, but you do not want to be injured so seriously that you can never play again. Entrepreneurs leave entrepreneuring for a variety of reasons; however, premature *career exits* frequently involve severe financial pressures brought about because the personal financial loss suffered by the entrepreneur was too great.

Remember, multiple ventures are the rule, not the exception for most entrepreneurial careers. 11 Take a longer term perspective — like buying a new house, very few of us should make our dream house the first home we purchase. Some entrepreneurs fail and start again. Others don't fail outright, but decide to pursue other ventures that look more promising. Others succeed and still start additional ventures. In each case, making the right financial decisions is paramount. You need to take control of these decisions, and financial projections are a vital decision making tool. These decisions are too important to leave entirely to others, especially your accountant.

The Corridor Principle offers some very practical advice to potential and practicing entrepreneurs. For new entrepreneurs, it says that you should start your first venture as soon as you find a "reasonable" opportunity. A "reasonable" opportunity means one that:

- will allow you to survive economically for a sufficient amount of time until you find a better opportunity.
- is in an industry where the likelihood is high that many intersecting corridors exist that lead to new venture opportunities.
- is not "time intensive" but gives you ample time to explore new opportunities.

For existing entrepreneurs, the advice drawn from the Corridor Principle is more situational. It depends on your venture goals and the success you've experienced in achieving your goals. For instance, if you are a successful Lifestyle entrepreneur, the last thing you probably want to do is go charging down new venture corridors. Who needs the headache of new venture births? Similarly, you may be a High Growth entrepreneur who sees ample opportunities with your existing venture. Again you probably have no need to create another venture. However, there are entrepreneurs who want to realize a different kind of success. Their existing venture(s) may be doing well, yet they want to try something more or less ambitious. Perhaps they want "to cut back" and become a Lifestyle entrepreneur or move from being a Smaller High Profit entrepreneur to a High Growth entrepreneur. In addition, there are entrepreneurs who simply want to realize more success without necessarily changing their venture goals. I've encountered many entrepreneurs who just can't seem to get to the next sales level (e.g., from a $1 or 2 million business to a $10 million business) no matter how hard they try.

For those existing entrepreneurs seeking some kind of change, the Corridor Principle provides a possible answer — one that is quite different from the prevailing guidance. The existing advice can be summarized in three phrases: "Stick to your knitting," "Be persistent," or "Focus on your existing business with unrelenting tenacity." Sometimes these admonitions are right, but what the Corridor Principle suggests is that sometimes they are very wrong.

Yet many entrepreneurs, myself included, have been superbly conditioned to believe we must always "stick to our knitting." In doing so we fail to see and pursue other venture opportunities ... or, even worse, we fail to see there are no or very few venture corridors intersecting our existing venture pathway. Instead, the guilt sets in. Why can't we make this venture better or more successful in terms of whatever it is we want to achieve? We want to take control, but we can't.

Sometimes you can mine a mountain or a venture just so far. Then it's time to move on to another mountain. Knowing when to move along to another venture requires skill and time. It also requires the presence of new venture opportunities. Given the inevitable limitations of time, you need an approach and tools to evaluate new corridor opportunities. Not every corridor opportunity should be pursued. In fact, some should be avoided like the plague. The issue is to determine, in a timely and efficient way, if a particular corridor is one you should pursue.

Here, rapid assessment of a venture possibility and its financial implications is the province of an owner ... not a staffer or your accountant. *This ongoing need for opportunity assessment is the compelling reason for a "venture feasibility approach," entrepreneurial finance, and Ronstadt's FINANCIALS.*

What Price Failure?

I believe there is no real failure for anyone who tries to realize their entrepreneurial dream. There may be pain and suffering but these are not the same as failure. That dismal mantle, if it rests anywhere, resides with those who could and should have started a venture but never started one.

For those with the courage to create a venture, let me try to crystalize my message to you.

Ventures should not be marketing driven, but customer driven. This distinction may seem minor, even semantical to you, especially if you haven't lived through the entrepreneurial process. But the drive to identify, understand, and satisfy your customers is the wellspring of entrepreneurial success.

However, the reality of entrepreneurial life is that you cannot be exclusively customer driven. A dynamic process is at work as you pass through the Prestartup and Startup phases of your venture. It is one where your customer orientation influences and is influenced by the product features you decide are necessary and feasible. Similarly your product and customer orientations influence and are influenced by your ability to determine the resources that are needed and your ability to assemble them. Eventually your ability (or inability) to produce your product or service and deliver it to your customers impacts the issues of customer, product, and entrepreneurial finance. They are all tied together as they should be.

However, my experience tells me that *most new entrepreneurs are weakest in their customer orientation and their abilities to answer the key questions of Entrepreneurial Finance.* Consequently they fail to assemble the appropriate resources in a timely and cost effective way. For too many entrepreneurs, finance has remained an impenetrable wall ... for many good reasons. It is particularly impenetrable for people starting and operating the smaller ventures that are the heart of our economy. As owners, these people must allocate time to the issues of Entrepreneurial Finance if they are to succeed or increase their present success. Yet it is hard to justify such time when one keeps smashing into the hard wall of finance.

Hopefully this book has breached this wall and provides a passageway for you to a more successful entrepreneurial life. For who needs the needless pain and suffering of trying to bore through or climb over a impenetrable wall of financial mystery? To avoid financial pain and suffering, it's a good idea to ask periodically

1 How much money does my venture need?

2 When does my venture need this money?

3 What kind of money (debt or equity) should this money be?

4 Where should I look for this money?

5 How much is this money worth?

Hopefully I have helped to give you greater insight about when to ask these questions and how to answer them. But most of all, I hope you have the opportunity to ask them. At the beginning of this book, I started with quotes from Al Shapero and John Steinbeck and it seems a good way to end. I can't think of two wiser souls to light our way.

One day, Al said to me, "You know, Bob, what this country needs is more entrepreneurial failures — not less." What Al knew from his experiences with countless entrepreneurs is that from failure comes success and, for the many who start a new venture, a good share will never experience the sting of failure.

And John Steinbeck ...

"I feel that a man is a very important thing — maybe more important than a star. This is not theology. I have no bent toward gods. But I have a new love for that glittering instrument, the human soul. It is a lovely and unique thing in the universe. It is always attacked and never destroyed — because 'Thou mayest.'"

"Now, there are many millions in their sects and churches who feel the order, 'Do thou,' and throw their weight into obedience. And there are millions more who feel predestination in 'Thou shalt.' Nothing they may do can interfere with what will be. But 'Thou mayest'! Why that makes a man great, that gives him stature with the gods, for in his weakness and his filth and his murder of his brother he has still the great choice. He can choose his course and fight it through and win." [12]

Endnotes

1   Basic distinctions have been made between male versus female, minority versus non-minority, and immigrant versus non-immigrant. Each of these classifications have helped us to better understand entrepreneurship. A few of these examples are: a) Norman Smith's classification of "opportunistic" versus "craftsman" entrepreneurs, b) Arnold Cooper's identification and study of "incubator entrepreneurs," and c) Cooper and Dunkelberg's grouping of "growth," and "independent," and "craftsman" entrepreneurs.

2   Albert Shapero, "Numbers That Lie," *Inc. Magazine,* May 1981, p. 16.

3   The exact figure is .7% reported by Dun & Bradstreet. (61,000 "failures" among their database of nine million enterprises in 1986). However, this 61,000 includes not only bankruptcies but also those firms that closed operations and withdrew leaving unpaid debts or settled creditors for less than the full amount of their debts. See their "Business Failure Record," *Tiziana Mohoronic,* edition, New York, 1986, p. 2.

4   The calculation of 3% is based on 1982 data when government statistics show there were approximately 14,500,000 businesses (10.1 million proprietorships), based on IRS returns. It excludes approximately 2 million farm businesses plus businesses that did not file a tax report. See "U.S. Department of Commerce," *Statistical Abstract Of The United States,* p. 517. The number of discontinuances (400,000) is taken from *The State of Small Business: A Report Of The President,* 1984, U.S. Government Printing Office, Washington, D.C. (400,000/14,500,000=2.8%)

5   See David Birch, "The Class Of '82," *Inc. Magazine,* December, 1987 which traces the Inc. 500 of 1982. Of the 500 ventures, 16 were closed, 61 had "disappeared" for a 15% disappearance rate. Birch also reports a 24% national disappearance rate for the same five year period (1983-1987).

6   See my article "The Corridor Principle," *Journal of Business Venturing,* Winter, 1988, pp. 31-40.

7   See my article, "Exit Stage Left: Why Entrepreneurs End Their
    Entrepreneurial Careers Before Retirement," *Journal of Business
    Venturing,* Fall, 1986, p. 334.

8   "Exit Stage Left," *Op. Cit.,* p. 336.

9   Karl Vesper, *New Venture Strategy,* Prentice Hall, Englewood Cliffs, NJ,
    1980, summarized from Chapter Two, "Success and Failure Factors,"
    pp. 27-55.

10 The John Hendrick piece is reproduced in *Entrepreneurship, Text, Cases
    & Notes,* "How I Overcame the Handicap of a College Education,"
    Lord Publishing, Natick, MA, 1984, pp.161-164.

11 "The Corridor Principle," *Op. Cit.,* p. 35.

12 John Steinbeck, *East Of Eden,* The Viking Press, New York, 1952,
    p. 247.

Index
And About the Author

Index

About the Author

Bob Ronstadt has forged a unique career as an entrepreneur, entrepreneurship teacher, and active researcher in the emerging field of entrepreneurial studies. He has served as the *lead entrepreneur* of a fast-growing company, and has developed and taught new courses in entrepreneurship that tap state-of-the-art knowledge about new venture formation. And he has contributed to this knowledge base by authoring many articles and books on entrepreneurial careers, entrepreneurship education, networking, and other areas of entrepreneurship.

Bob received his Doctorate in Business Administration from the Harvard Business School in 1975, and until recently, has pursued a dual career as a business educator and entrepreneur. In 1976, Bob and his wife Rebecca, co-founded Lord Publishing. In 1985, he won The Freedom Foundation's Leavey Award for Excellence in Private Enterprise Education. This prestigious award was presented to him for the development of Babson College's Academic Program in Entrepreneurship, and for his widely adopted book entitled *Entrepreneurship: Text, Cases and Notes*.

In 1986, he expanded and refocused Lord Publishing to provide a range of new products for entrepreneurs and business owners that would improve their chances for venture success. And in 1987, he left a tenured position at Babson College to devote full time to this pursuit.

Entrepreneurial Finance is only one of a fine family of Lord Publishing Inc.'s books and software products designed to assist entrepreneurs, managers, and financial decision makers. Other products include:

LORD PUBLISHING, INC.
Suite 320
One Apple Hill
Natick, MA 01760
1-800-525-5673
(in MA, 508-651-9955)

Ronstadt's Financials™ for doing financial projections, budgeting, and analysis... fast and easy. A revolutionary software package for IBM PCs and compatibles. The statement-driven program is an expert system that gives decision makers control over their financial decisions. It is a stand-alone program that, in minutes, generates a complete set of financial projections without the struggle of trying to use spreadsheet programs or outside professionals.

Venture Feasibility Planning Guide: Your First Step Before Writing A Business Plan. This workbook is a step-by-step guide that helps entrepreneurs and planners focus and evaluate potential ventures before writing the business plan.

The Business Plan: A State-of-the-Art Guide. A comprehensive guide on how to write a business plan of professional caliber. Proves that good business plan workbooks don't have to be expensive.

Entrepreneurship: Text, Cases, and Notes. The textbook of choice for entrepreneurship in the '80s. Required text at colleges, business schools, universities, and corporate management training groups.

Networking for Success: Know-Who Plus Know-How. This guide elaborates on the ten rules for establishing and utilizing valuable contacts in your personal and professional networks.

Yes, I want to know more about taking control of my financial decision making. Please tell me more about Lord Publishing's fine family of products.

_____
Name   Title

_____
Company

_____
Address

_____
City   State   Zip

_____
Phone

❏ **Ronstadt's Financials (The Software)**

❏ **Ronstadt's Financials Trial Pack**   _($9.95 enclosed)_

❏ **Entrepreneurial Finance**   _hardcover ($32.95)   softcover ($16.95)_

❏ **Venture Feasibility Planning Guide**   _($19.95)_

❏ **The Business Plan: A State-of-the-Art Guide**   _($29.95)_

❏ **Entrepreneurship: Text, Cases, and Notes**   _($32.95)_

❏ **Networking For Success: Know-who Plus Know-How**   _($2.50)_

Lord Publishing, Inc.
One Apple Hill
Suite 320
Natick, MA 01760